Still Flying Full Throttle!

The Continuing Story of the DeMerchants in the Amazon

Still Flying
Full
Throttle!

The Continuing Story of the DeMerchants in the Amazon

Bennie DeMerchant
Dolly McElhaney

WORD AFLAME PRESS
HAZELWOOD, MO

Still Flying Full Throttle
The Continuing Story of the DeMerchants in the Amazon

© 2015 by Bennie DeMerchant and Dolly McElhaney

Printed in the United States of America.

Printed by

WORD AFLAME PRESS
8855 Dunn Road, Hazelwood, MO 63042
www.pentecostalpublishing.com

Library of Congress Cataloging-in-Publication Data

McElhaney, Dolly.
  Still flying full throttle : the continuing story of the DeMerchants in the Amazon / by Dolly McElhaney.
    pages cm
  ISBN 978-0-7577-4706-9 (alk. paper)
  1. DeMerchant, Bennie, 1941- 2. DeMerchant, Theresa. 3. Missionaries--Brazil--Biography. 4. Missionaries--United States--Biography. 5. United Pentecostal Church International--Missions--Brazil. 6. Indians of South America--Brazil--Missions. 7. Waimiri Indians--Missions. I. Title.
  BV2853.B7A1353 2015
  266'.9940922--dc23
  [B]

                                                2015021564

*With great appreciation,
we dedicate this book to our friends,
Rev. Gerald and Eleanor Grant,
who have worked together over sixty years
helping mold thousands of disciples
as president and teachers
at the Apostolic Bible Institute
in Saint Paul, Minnesota.*

*Bennie and Theresa DeMerchant
Manaus, Brazil
May 2015*

Contents

Preface

In *Full Throttle: The Missionary Story of Bennie and Theresa DeMerchant in the Amazon*, Bennie DeMerchant posed a question that was never answered. The question, "Can these wild Indians ever be reached with the life-changing message of Jesus Christ?" begged for a response. This book, *Still Flying Full Throttle*, responds to that question.

The stories in this book are all new. In 2008 while I attended my fiftieth anniversary graduation from the Apostolic Bible Institute in St. Paul, Minnesota, Brother Gerald Grant said to me, "Dolly, if I had known you were writing a book about Brother DeMerchant, I would have given you access to all the letters he wrote me."

I immediately coveted those letters!

Brother Grant agreed to my request for copies of those letters. Some of the original material Brother DeMerchant had sent me as a basis for *Full Throttle* had gone unused. That earlier material plus the information in Brother Grant's letters would easily comprise a second book.

At the time of my request, Bethany Sievers, the DeMerchants' granddaughter, was a senior at ABI. She copied the letters, put them into notebooks, and then sent them to me. All six of them. I was astonished at what my sin of covetousness had wrought!

Many of the letters contained requests for airplane parts or technical details concerning flying a floatplane. After these pages were culled from the letters, five notebooks of material remained. The stories in *Still Flying Full Throttle* were extracted from the remaining letters, which began in 1969 and ended in 1996 when the Internet entered the picture and email took the place of snail mail.

After *Full Throttle* was published, the DeMerchants

and I stayed in contact with each other. Seeing that there were two significant areas not adequately covered in *Full Throttle*, I saved and printed out every email they sent me. Those areas—the incursion into Indian tribes and the expansion abroad—needed to be investigated and the results reported.

Still Flying Full Throttle brings the reader from 1969 up to the present time, and answers the question about those "wild Indians."

Dolly McElhaney
Cookeville, Tennessee
April 2015

Acknowledgments

In grateful appreciation for necessary help, I admiringly salute

Gerald Grant, who revealed to me that he still had hundreds of letters from Bennie DeMerchant and offered to let me have copies of them;

Bethany Sievers for so patiently photocopying page after page of letters from her grandfather to Gerald Grant, all six legal-sized notebooks crammed with them;

Jonas Pinto for straightening me out on details of the story in which he took part;

Those wonderful young people from the First United Pentecostal Church in Cookeville: Micah Abner, Kacey Delafontaine, Olivia Gonzales, Lacie Green, Sarah Green, Tyler Green, Gabe Litchford, Joshua Roman, Samuel Sullivan, Catherine Sullivan, Emily Sullivan, Gregory Truitt, and Rodney Truitt, Jr. These exemplary young people traded an afternoon of diligent work for a few pizzas and the promise of an autographed copy of this book;

Sally Spite, a dear sister in the Lord who gave time, critical comment, and a big boost when I needed it badly;

Courtney Edmonds for extending to me her expertise in everything computer-wise by snagging pictures from Facebook and a disk when even my husband, Bill, couldn't solve the problems;

Daniel Borges, fine young translator-into-Portuguese for that version of *Full Throttle Two*, as we dubbed it;

Brothers Buford and Gossard at PPH for putting up with my questions and giving me respectful, considerate answers;

Bill McElhaney, my husband of fifty-six years (he deserves sainthood for just that one thing alone) who supports me and gives me necessary (though at times unwelcome), criticism and unending, unswerving support and love; and

To the Lord Jesus, who rather unexpectedly gave me the opportunity and privilege of chronicling the part of the 29th chapter of Acts happening in Brazil,

Thank you times ten!
Dolly McElhaney
Cookeville, Tennessee
April 2015

1 Culture Clash

Bennie DeMerchant rolled and tossed, trying to sleep. When he closed his eyes, however, all he could see were the ravaged bodies of the victims of the Atroari Indians' latest killing spree, and he couldn't erase the grisly pictures from his mind.

Earlier that day, Bennie, missionary and pilot, had flown Gilberto Figueredo and another Brazilian government agent north to a jungle outpost on the crossing point of a projected highway over the Alalaú River to investigate a report they had received. Operated by National Foundation for the Indians (FUNAI) personnel from Manaus, they hoped to befriend the Waimiri-Atroari Indians when they appeared. After landing and tethering his floatplane, Bennie had inched along the trunk of a tree fallen onto the riverbank as he followed Gilberto and the other agent to the site of the Atroari massacre—the fourth that year.

Gilberto's job as liaison between the government and the various Indian tribes was to pacify the Indians so the government could build a road through their territory from Manaus north to Boa Vista, a town near the Venezuelan border. The Trans-Amazon Highway had to traverse the high ground in Indian territory. The more direct route lay to the west along the Rio Negro and Rio Branco, but it was a vast swampy area.

Of the four men stationed at the government outpost, three had died there. One body, consisting of skull, a section of vertebrae, and bits of arm and leg bones, lay only a few feet from the ashes of the outpost. The fourth man had barely escaped by swimming across the river, hiding in the jungle, and following the road to Manaus. As soon as he reached the city, he reported the massacre to his superiors at FUNAI.

Bennie couldn't sleep with this scene seared into his brain, playing before his eyes over and over. *Is it really February 3, 1973?* he wondered. *Will we ever be able to reach such treacherous, murderous people with the saving, life-changing gospel of Jesus Christ?*

A few months later, Bennie flew in to the same post to pick up a road engineer who wanted to get some kind of a position from the sun with his equipment. At Gilberto's suggestion a few weeks after that, Bennie took his wife, Theresa, and their two little girls, Beth and Pam, for a friendly visit to the outpost to show he was a family man with a wife and children. At the end of June, he flew Gilberto and two of the Indian chiefs to the Indian Foundation Headquarters in Manaus for a two-day visit to introduce them to civilization. When Bennie flew the Indians back to their outpost, all seemed well.

It was—for a while.

The Foundation received word of yet another Indian attack at the Alalaú River outpost. The Indians had come in to the outpost and asked three of the men there to go on a hunting trip. A few hundred feet from the outpost in the jungle, the Indians put arrows into the backs of two of the men. The third agent pulled his revolver and fired into the air, scaring the Indians. As he fled, the Indians shot an arrow with such force through the top of his kidney that the arrow protruded from the front, with the feathers inside the man.

The Indians who had stayed behind attacked the remaining three employees. One man had been standing in the doorway drinking fruit juice when an Indian sneaked up behind him and beheaded him with a violent slash of a machete. The Indians killed the others by arrows and tossed their bodies into the river. After pounding the metal shell of the radio, the Indians took off with an outboard motor and three canoes.

The man with the arrow sticking out of him crawled to the road right-of-way where highway workers found him. They managed to get him into a jeep and drive to a hospital in Manaus, where he died two days later.

"One can never tell what these savages are thinking," Bennie wrote to his long-time friend, Gerald Grant. "Even their kids are dangerous with a bow and arrow up to fifty yards away. I put two tons of food for the Army on the Alalaú River canteen—rice, flour, sugar, oil—and the Indians attacked again, killing the four men who were taking care of the canteen."

Months later, in the late fall of 1974, a horrified Bennie would stare at blood-red headlines in *A Noticia*, Manaus's daily newspaper: "The Atroaris Kill Gilberto."

Just three weeks earlier, Bennie had left Gilberto at the Abonari River outpost. His caution still rang in his head.

"Gilberto, be very careful," Bennie had warned. "You have lost a lot of men this summer in three ambushes that ended in massacres."

"Pastor Bennie, I know these Indians and they trust me," Gilberto had replied.

These friendly, trusting Indians had shot eight arrows into Gilberto's back and three more into his chest. Reading the newspaper account, Bennie wondered again if the gospel would ever reach the Atroaris, especially since atheist anthropologists influenced government policy to leave the Indians with their own culture and to keep mission societies out.

Bennie and Theresa DeMerchant had been United Pentecostal Church missionaries in Manaus, Brazil, since October 1965. Each had been wonderfully fashioned by God with skills, talents, and interests they would need on the mission field, and each had received a calling from God to be a missionary to Brazil. Their lives had touched each other when they met at the Apostolic Bible Institute in St. Paul, Minnesota, and then became intertwined when they were married in July 1961.

After pastoring in New Brunswick, Canada, for two years, they traveled to Memphis, Tennessee, to attend the General Conference of the United Pentecostal Church International. There they applied to be appointed to Brazil as missionaries. Refused on their first application, they reapplied the following year in San Antonio, Texas.

They waited nervously outside a meeting room with Pauline Gruse from Liberia, and evangelists Sam and Joyce Latta. When the Foreign Missions secretary Paul Box opened the door, they walked in before the other board members: Oscar Vouga, director of Foreign Misions; Hulon Myre, A. D. Gurley, Jewel Cole, Edwin Judd, W. J. Rolston, R. G. Cook, and V. A. Shoemake.

These men had all read the DeMerchants' application information and held yes or no power in their hands.

"These young people come from a great Pentecostal upbringing," Brother Vouga said in support of their petition. "I've already talked with them."

Others, however, expressed objections.

"Maybe if these folks are willing to live and work for a couple of years under Samuel Baker in São Paulo, we could send them," someone said.

"The heat and humidity of Manaus would be a difficult

environmental adjustment after cold Canada," another minister pointed out.

At each comment, Bennie's heart dropped a notch, but when R. G. Cook asked him how old he was, his spirit plummeted.

"I am twenty-three," he answered, thinking, *I must look like an overgrown teenager. Am I going to have to face the Board again at next year's conference?* Bennie knew that Billy Cole had been on the mission field in Thailand when he was twenty-eight years old, but it seemed like a long shot for Bennie at the age of twenty-three. At least, Bennie could explain before the Lord in prayer that he had tried, twice.

Brother Vouga leaned back in his chair. "Brethren, we have sent men to the field who were too long in the ministry in the US. Their children were already in their teens. They had problems learning a foreign language and adjusting to an adverse culture. Maybe it's time to drop down to younger missionary candidates."

Bennie's spirit perked up.

Then the Board turned their searchlight on Theresa. Always poised in the middle of any storm, Theresa calmly answered their questions about going to a strange land and bringing up her children there in the heat, humidity, and disease. They studied her and balanced among them the big question: Will these young people, only in their twenties, stay on the field?

The Missionary Board of the United Pentecostal Church decided they could. Bennie and Theresa were at last appointed as missionaries to Brazil!

The building couldn't contain their elation. Bennie opened the back door and walked outside. On the opposite side of the street farther down, he spied a Western Union Telegraph office sign. He strode down the San Antonio street toward it and entered it while the teletype machines were banging away.

"I want to send a message," he said, and on the message pad wrote, "Mom! We were appointed to Brazil in the General Conference TODAY!"

Four other couples, the Cobbs, the Millers, the Lattas, and the Bernards were also appointed in that evening's service.

After a year of preparation, the DeMerchants arrived in Manaus, Brazil, in October 1965, smack in the middle of the Amazon Basin. Sam Baker, their missionary supervisor from São Paulo, helped them for five days, staying at the Amazonas Hotel and checking newspaper ads to find a house to rent and settle into.

They spent hours on their faces before God, beseeching Him for souls. For many weeks they immersed themselves in the Portuguese language. After fourteen months of concentrated study, Bennie felt his fluency in the language would allow him to preach his first sermon.

Their first four-year missionary term saw them struggling to establish a church despite sauna-like, strength-sapping heat; Brazilian families constantly relocating to find better jobs; soccer games, as important to Brazilians as breath; Carnival and a multitude of other religious holidays and festivals; often insufficient funds; and no helpers. Manaus, being only three degrees south of the equator and only 150 feet above sea level, remains very hot and humid most of the year. They had come to minister in a place where breathing was like drawing air in from a furnace.

They persevered. They not only established a church in Manaus, they reached out to neighboring towns. Near the end of their first term, in late June 1969, Bennie wrote to his friend, Gerald Grant, in Saint Paul, Minnesota,

The work continues to grow. Baptized four more this month. One-God messages reach out each Sunday on Radio Bare. The local church in Manaus is sending Brother Manual Bizerra and family to open a work in Manacapuru, an interior town of 4,000. This Jesus-name baptized brother worked in the interior for several years. We believe he will do a good work. Our local church bought a lot there and we have raised a wooden frame building covered with aluminum sheet roofing and we expect to get the cement floor finished soon.

The Brazilian way of doing business seemed extremely inefficient. Personal service was an unknown concept. A parcel of clothes had arrived in Manaus for them in March, and almost every day since then Bennie had gone to the customs house trying to get it released. The enervating heat, carelessness, and disinterest would make one man put the request off on the other man's desk till it landed on the desk of someone who was out on vacation and remained there till he returned, only to be transferred to another elsewhere.

In another example, Bennie worked for two months to transfer the deed on their central church lot and it seemed no closer to being finalized than when he started. There were thirty departments in the courthouse through which the request for transference had to pass before being released with all the signatures and stamps on it. Things were backward and years behind the times.

"We can't paint our house here or dig a sewer or build without a license from the courthouse which takes 60-90 days to acquire," Bennie explained. "We would have left here long ago, discouraged with all this red tape if it hadn't been for the call of God which keeps us content, and for the joy we feel when precious souls are baptized in Jesus' name and filled with His Spirit." Though this slow, unorganized way of life frustrated them at every turn, it also challenged them to build a strong central church that Jesus might take out a people for His name when He comes back.

In spite of all the hindrances, by the end of their first term as missionaries, Bennie and Theresa had established two churches of solid, Jesus Name baptized, Holy Ghost filled believers: one in Manaus in Santo Antonio, west of downtown, and another on Avenida Presidente Castelo Branco near their home. They had reached into the jungle to start a house church on Marrecão Island, sixty miles west of Manaus. They were building an apartment for the help that was coming at last in the person of Margaret Calhoun, a trained teacher who loved kids and had a heart for God.

They had also tried to start churches in the Moro de Liberdade and São Francisco suburbs in Manaus, but had no workers to carry them on. When they saw that the two of them were not doing well, they let the rented one go and sold the other.

The geography of the region presented their biggest drawback to expansion. The Amazon River stretches from the Andes Mountains of Peru on the west (where it is called the Solimões) to the Atlantic Ocean on the east. Manaus bisects its two thousand mile length where the mighty Rio Negro disgorges its flow into the river and where its name changes to Amazon. The westernmost Brazilian town on the mighty river is Tabatinga on the Peruvian-Colombian-Brazilian border; the easternmost is Macapá. Many of the tributaries to the Amazon are long, impossibly convoluted rivers with fast currents in the rainy season.

These rivers uncoil throughout the jungle with sweeping hairpin or clover-leaf turns one after another as far as the eye can see from the air. Sometimes boats would chug away navigating these huge loops and come back to within a few hundred feet from where they had been just hours before.

Although two thousand miles of river flow beneath a flying crow's wings, the hundreds of loops in its serpentine course add another two thousand miles to its length! Manaus perches about halfway between Tabatinga and Macapá. So how in the world could one young couple evangelize a nearly roadless area three-fourths the size of the continental United States?

The obvious answer? Only by plane. And only by floatplane.

Within a mile of this road sign, Bennie DeMerchant was born on January 31, 1941, in South Tilly, New Brunswick, Canada.

On the left, Bennie's parents, Harold and Beatrice DeMerchant; on the right, uncle Herman Taylor

21

Plaster Rock, New Brunswick, the church the
DeMerchants left behind for Brazil

Bea DeMerchant, sixteen years old

Beyond the Back of Beyond

As a teenager, Bennie had worked to save money for flying lessons. At ABI in St. Paul, he had often flown with his friend, Gerald Grant. So Bennie decided to try for a Brazilian pilot's license. He took the tests written in Portuguese at the Ponta Pelada airport when Brazil's Department of Aeronautics examiners came from Rio de Janeiro. To keep up on his flying skills, Bennie joined the local Aero-club on Flores airstrip north of the city.

He flew for an hour or two every month in the flying club's airplanes but began to shy away from them after a scary incident. One day Bennie took a church friend up for a ride in a Paulistinha, a canvas-covered trainer two-seater wheel plane. They flew out over the city, past the meeting of the Amazon and Negro Rivers and away from the town toward the jungle. Flying along at about three thousand feet, they decided to do some maneuvering with the plane. Bennie cut the power back to idle and let the plane slow down. The engine did more than idle—it quit altogether! The plane glided slowly in silence except for the sound of the wind. The propeller had stopped in mid-air and the aircraft had no electrical system with a starter. It had been started by hand swinging the prop on the ground.

Bennie spotted a pool of calm water in the Amazon River near the jungle's edge where he could put the plane down and they could swim for shore, but they would lose the little bird! They still had good altitude but he dared wait no longer to try his one hope of restarting the engine. He pushed the nose down to build up air speed. The propeller swung in the air—and stopped.

"You've gotta' go on over, boy!" Bennie exclaimed, his heart in his throat. He pushed the nose steeper still until the wind whistled outside and the light aircraft began to quiver and shake as it plunged almost straight down toward the river. Slowly the propeller edged around once, then twice. With more momentum, the propeller's rotation gradually increased while Bennie pumped the throttle. They had a live engine again!

The engine caught at only eight hundred feet above the Amazon River. Bennie pulled the nose up and they leveled out of their dive. As they headed back to the airport the little plane quit quivering, but when Bennie taxied the plane back to the small hangar and got out, his legs still trembled. Somewhat shakily, he told the mechanic that the engine had stopped during a slow flight a few minutes earlier.

"We have no brake linings for the plane's wheels," the mechanic explained. "The wheel linings are worn out and the plane has so little braking that I adjusted the idling engine as low as possible so it would not advance. That lets the headwind stop the plane when it lands."

Bennie suggested to the mechanic to wait for the linings to arrive or adjust the idling up before he rented the plane out again. "Someday a student pilot might get in trouble in a similar situation," he cautioned.

During 1970, the DeMerchants returned to the US for their first furlough and to visit the churches that had supported their mission to Brazil. Then in June 1971, the

Foreign Missions Department, realizing the watery-ness of the Amazon Basin, provided them with their greatest need to adequately evangelize the northern portion of Brazil: a Cessna 172 floatplane registered as PT-ICQ. Bennie flew the little bird from the United States to Manaus while Theresa and their two girls traveled on a commercial flight.

While the DeMerchants were traveling on deputation, Margaret Calhoun had anchored their home and mission in Manaus. She had won a tall, strong, young man to the Lord. Jonas Pinto worked with her and other workers in Autazes during the DeMerchants' 1970-71 furlough and went to Bible school the next year. When he returned, he and Margaret held street meetings in Autazes, a town across the Amazon on the banks of the Madeirinha (little Madeira) River on a 160-mile-long island about seventy-five miles southeast of Manaus. The group of believers multiplied, and before long they bought a lot and built a church. Eager to spread this gospel still farther, Jonas longed to check out Maués, a town even farther east. The DeMerchants were excited about this extension of their mission.

Bennie and Jonas found a small group of believers in Maués who asked the two men to preach for them. Their pastor had warned them not to listen to Bennie and Jonas, so of course the Brazilians then wanted to hear them even more. When Jonas yearned to open a work there, Bennie encouraged him to do so. Between October 1972 and July 1973, Bennie made twenty flights to Maués to help Jonas.

In early January 1973, Bennie wrote to Gerald Grant:

> I was down to Maués for weekend services. All seems to be going well there. Jonas is working with two churches. Work continues to grow. People there are very poor. Ninety percent of the houses are built with clay floors. All they

needed was someone to stay there and teach and guide and organize and build a church. I believe if we had a boat and motor for Jonas and a church building of about 22' x 50', we could have a few hundred members in three or four months.

Bennie and Jonas purchased an aluminum boat and motor for church work. They decided that after Jonas had the work in Maués firmly established, Jonas could use the boat to follow leads along the river to evangelize rural areas. Jonas stashed all his belongings and supplies in the newly acquired boat. The riverboat crew hoisted it onto the flat, wooden, zinc-covered canopy where empty drums, mattresses, Styrofoam ice boxes and other light, bulky items were carried.

All went well that night until the captain switched to the other side of the Amazon for straighter navigation. After the boat moved away from the protection of the shore and out into the middle of the river, crosswinds and waves caused the craft to roll. The boat started rocking, the canopy top started swaying, and Jonas, in his hammock, heard the aluminum boat slide over the side nose down in an almost vertical fall. When Jonas swung out of his hammock to look, all he saw was the bow of the canoe easing under the water. In their hurry to load the boat, they had forgotten to tie the canoe on! Even worse, the boat factory had neglected to put Styrofoam in the rectangular seat compartments to make the canoe buoyant if it filled with water.

A terribly discouraged Jonas prayed earnestly after losing the canoe. Suddenly a man in white clothes appeared on the boat inside the canvas stretched down over the side to protect the hammocks during rain.

"Yes, you made the mistake of not tying the boat on and it is a great loss to you," the man told Jonas, "but Bennie would not consider its value against the opportunity you will have in Maués. Just continue on your trip."

Jonas told Bennie later that the man lifted the canvas and straddled the side of the boat as if he were stepping down into a canoe alongside. After a few seconds Jonas wanted to see what kind of boat the man had come in, so he lifted the canvas and looked on every side. It was day time by then, but he saw no boat in sight anywhere in the middle of the Amazon River!

When Jonas made his first phone contact with Bennie, he was distraught. "Pastor Bennie," he cried. "Let me come back to Manaus and find a job so I can pay for the canoe."

Bennie told him almost word for word what the man in white had said. "The boat is nothing compared to the mission, so continue on with your plan of reaching Maués and the many rural locations on lakes, rivers, and backwaters. Just play it cool. The devil is against our going into Maués, and all that happened is an indication of his opposition. A great revival is waiting there, so just keep to your plan."

Later, Bennie took Theresa, Beth, and little Pam to Maués one Sunday and helped Jonas baptize seventy-three people in one day. Together they laughed about the canoe on the bottom of the Amazon. It is probably still there, filled with mud from the bottom wash of the river.

At that time, the government was building a road north from Manaus to Boa Vista near the Venezuelan border. The road contractors or military workers received dried food and medications in tensile pill packets; any unbreakable items were sewn into packed fiber bags pitched out from a wheeled plane. As the road stretched farther and farther away from Manaus, the road right-of-way became too narrow between the trees. Crosswinds caught one of their planes; it got so banged up that the government decided to quit flights to the area using wheeled planes.

The government turned to Bennie for help. Bennie didn't like to throw stuff out of the plane but there was no other way to get supplies to the men. Without the door on, wind swirled through the opening. A man anchored one end of a cord around the flooring hooks near the pilot's seat and the other end around his waist in case he might slip when throwing stuff out. He stayed inside seated on the floor with a foot on an outside horizontal bar above the floats and tossed items from the plane. Imagine what a sack of rice would do when filled to the brim and sewn up, thrown out of a plane going 80 mph, dropping one hundred feet and hitting a tree stump! Much of the food was lost until one day Bennie suggested they put only half the usual amount in a bag and then insert that bag inside another bag. "Then if it hits a tree stump, half a bag won't break on impact but the contents will have enough space to spread out," Bennie explained.

After that, they lost very little of the things they threw out.

During this time, Bennie first saw Indians on surveying overflights to the north. Then he met them face to face. He reported to Gerald:

> They are in another world. I went in with Gilberto Figueredo, the state director of the National Foundation for the Indians (FUNAI). Saw some 11 commune houses and photographed them from the air. When I landed the plane, so many Indians got on the float that it temporarily sank, so they jumped off into their dugout canoe on the side. Except for a waist vine that they tie around them they are completely naked. Bronze

skin with long black hair cut like they put a large bowl over their head, and no beard.

Financing the airplane—fuel, maintenance, and parts—was boosted by flights the Brazilian government requested. When a colonel and his wife disappeared on the river and had been missing for two days, the army asked Bennie to help find the couple. For over five hours, Bennie scoured the many ins and outs of the Rio Negro archipelago above Manaus. The twenty-mile-wide river winds in and out of dozens of long finger-like islands. A guide or knowledgeable person is needed to help navigate such trips as the colonel and his wife took, because in the dry season with no current to indicate direction, everything looks the same. Finally spotting them in a broken-down diesel boat, Bennie splashed down beside them, handed them food and sodas, and reported back to the military. Bennie had donated his time, but the military gave him a plastic card for authorization to use their military port in the middle of Manaus at any time. The card also allowed him to use any army truck to haul gasoline to the floating hangar where he kept his plane.

A few days later, Bennie took a couple of drums of gas to a barge to dispatch it about 750 air miles (1,500 river miles) southwest to Eirunepé on the River Juruá. Some saints on Marrecão, an island near Manacapuru, had relatives in Eirunepé, and wanted them to hear about baptism in Jesus' name and being filled with the Holy Ghost, so he planned to go there in February. Aviation gas was scarce there. By sending the fuel to his destination by river, Bennie wouldn't have to buy fuel at double or triple the price (if it were available at all) hundreds of miles away when coming or going with a loaded plane.

Finally, in March 1973, Bennie spread his wings southwest toward Eirunepé in this new venture, the

29

farthest from Manaus he'd yet flown. He took two workers with him. As usual, he had stocked the plane with books, tracts, and hammocks. Bennie and his helpers wanted to set up a brush arbor and hold services, but time wouldn't let him do that. A layman in charge of the services in a local church asked them to preach because their pastor was away. They preached to a full house! Bennie noted the folks in the congregation shouted a lot, but he wondered if they would ever be baptized in the name of Jesus. He passed out a lot of literature and left the two workers with their relatives. They would be directing services every night for a month.

On the way back to Manaus, he landed in Lábrea to eat dinner. Two priests, a nun, and a bishop in the Roman Catholic Church from Bogotá, Colombia, met him on the shore and requested a ride to Manaus. They were still waiting by the plane even after he had eaten dinner at a restaurant. Bennie really had no reason to say no, especially with half the town watching him, so he told them to climb in but advised them that he couldn't take off with more than 440 pounds of weight. The bishop weighed at least 250 pounds. He squeezed in. The other priests were skinny fellows, and one clambered in clutching three suitcases. That left one thin priest and a small nun that Bennie felt sorry for standing on the riverbank.

Bennie reports it this way: "I said to myself, 'Boy, I'm not taking this load to Manaus.' I knew I could get off if I wanted it to work but I held full throttle for a couple of short runs with the heels digging in (on purpose) so it wouldn't climb up on the step, and told them it was impossible to get them to Manaus because they were too heavy."

At Lábrea, the plane's gas tanks held only an hour of fuel to fly to the next stop. From there Bennie would need five hours' worth of fuel to reach Manaus. The heavily loaded plane, if caught in bad weather, might force a dangerous landing on the river. Bennie felt it best to leave them in their home setting in Lábrea than to risk a problem in the boonies farther down.

The heavy-set bishop, in getting into a small canoe, nearly sank it. Bennie flew the slim priest and little nun back to Manaus through a violent storm that tossed the light 172 about through rain that beat against it while the priest called upon all the saints he could think of. Bennie, busy with piloting the little plane, thought of the overload the bishop, priests, and baggage could have caused and was happy he'd left them safe and dry in Lábrea. They landed in Manaus without further incident.

A few weeks later Bennie flew back to Eirunepé to pick up the workers he'd left there the previous month. On the return to Manaus, Bennie set down in Foz do Jutai, a town of about one thousand inhabitants. Men were busy with transits, laying out a water system for the town. As Bennie secured the plane, the mayor approached him.

"Please come and start a church here," the mayor begged. "Walk around and pick out an unoccupied lot. I'll check it out and donate the land to you. We have neither church nor priest. I listen to the Voice of the Andes on shortwave every night and sure do like that music."

Town mayors frequently made offers of that kind. The mayor knew that a mission operating an airplane on wheels or on floats could benefit the small town greatly. Medicines or vaccines on ice could be obtained more rapidly, and hospital services in a larger city would become available.

Reluctantly, Bennie shook his head. "We'll have to consider it for future growth," he said. "We don't have the men at the present." It hurt—having to refuse the offer of land and turning his back on evangelizing a place where he and the workers would be welcome. But the place was five and a half hours of flight time from Manaus, and he had in mind a larger town that was in a direct route beyond

Eirunepé toward the headwaters of the crooked Juruá River. He intended to scout out that back-of-the-beyond place as soon as he could.

Theresa Shomberg at Apostolic Bible Institute, 1960

Bennie and Gerald Grant in St. Paul, Minnesota, 1960

The Fertile Crescent

Bennie's destination was Cruzeiro do Sul, a town of 25,000 to 30,000 people beyond Eirunepé and closer to the headwaters of the river he followed in Brazil's far southwestern corner near Peru. As he flew along the crooked, muddy Juruá River for safety, the green rainforest stretched to the horizon on all sides. If all went well, tugboats with barges from Manaus could navigate rivers for forty days and nights in the rainy season to bring heavy cargo, including precious aviation fuel, to this remote city unreachable by road. It was 1973 and Bennie wanted to plant a church there for the name of Jesus. But first he needed to scout out the place.

At last the town loomed on the horizon and Bennie dropped the nose of the 172 toward the river that formed one side of the town. He taxied along on the water looking for a safe place to tie up the airplane. Huge dugout canoes noisily plowed the brown waters on each side of the seaplane, their four-cycle engines turning on a transom pin under the long shaft of a propeller. These canoes delivered passengers, livestock, and groceries to and from dwellings along this serpentine river. Ahead, larger boats with high, oval-roof canopies were tied side by side, blocking any possibility that his winged boat could join them in their tight-fitting "parking lot." However, beyond them lay a low, flat beach with high bushes nearby that seemed the ideal choice to tie up his Cessna seaplane to weather any night storm. Bennie noticed curious folks staring down at him from the high riverbank.

Three plane lengths from shore Bennie cut the engine to idle, then coasted to a soft stop. With river current pushing on one side threatening to slide the plane back into the mainstream of the river, he had to move fast. Quickly unbuckling his safety belt, he grabbed a coiled rope, opened the door, and stepped onto the pontoon. Ducking under the wing strut, he ran to the front, dropped a loop of rope around the pontoon's front cleat and with the other end of the rope in hand, leapt for the shore.

What a tremendous shock to discover the beach was quicksand! When Bennie stopped sinking, the water leveled with his belt. The crowd on the upper bank roared with laughter. Now Bennie realized why no boats had docked at this spot.

Hundreds of curious spectators peered down at him. They had never seen an airplane maneuvering on the water. They had never seen a pilot floundering in the muck. What a show! Bennie felt as if he were on television. Every time he moved in the mud he sank deeper. Pulling one leg higher only sucked the other leg down that much more. The bank crowd howled with every move he made, laughing again and again.

Bennie had learned to talk to himself positively when in trouble, so he consoled himself by thinking of worse situations. *At least I am not up flying in bad weather,* he thought, *nearly out of gas with night coming on.*

Then a voice whispered in his ear, mocking him. "And you are going to start a new church in this city? It will never happen! Go home! You are the laughingstock of the town!"

A dugout canoe eased up alongside of him. Its owner dropped a flat, wide board under Bennie's arm and told him to work himself out of the mud up onto it. Time stretched into an eternity as Bennie wallowed about in the mire and splashed in the muddied water, but he finally rolled into the canoe. The canoe owner dug out Bennie's shoes and washed the muck off. What a public display of incompetence Bennie had shown to the whole town!

After Bennie got out of the mud, the friendly canoeist took him into the river where he could wash from top to bottom. The boat fellow returned Bennie to the plane where he retrieved his overnight things and tied up the plane in that good spot. No one would mess with it there! The friendly canoeist paddled to another spot where Bennie stepped out of the canoe on solid ground. He climbed up over the bank where some people greeted him. They had never met a pilot and were very curious about him.

As Bennie strolled around Cruzeiro do Sul and peered into its shops, he sensed these were people who dealt with the raw side of life. He greeted many people and in shaking their hands felt callouses on their palms and fingers, an indication that they worked hard to survive. Bennie knew such folks readily received the gospel and that after a tremendous experience with God, they would labor diligently in His cause. With training they would be unlimited in their accomplishments. Bennie's mouth watered for the day when they would have a stable work going here in the westernmost part of Brazil.

By May, the workers downriver from Cruzeiro do Sul in Eirunepé had harvested enough souls that they needed a building in which to worship. Another floating church was being built in the Maués area. A woman, Sister Faustina, had started a work in a rural area of Maués, later turned it over to the Brazilian church, and moved west to

Itacoatiara. She had a group of believers there and asked Bennie to "hop" over and preach.

One Sunday morning after Bennie ferried people from Maués to Parintins to Manaus, the mayor and a medical doctor came to the church. Bennie was on the platform about to speak when an usher handed him a message that they wanted to talk with him. Bennie turned the service over to the pastor and walked toward them. Outside the church door, they explained their summons.

"We have a woman in serious trouble," they said. "She must get to the hospital in Itacoatiara."

With an intravenous bottle hanging from the ceiling and the medical student in attendance, Bennie flew the woman to Itacoatiara. He had hardly returned home and was preparing for evening service when another call arose.

"Bennie, we have a man who was in a motorcycle accident and broke his thigh bone," came the request.

As Bennie prepared for another mercy flight that day, he knew the Sunday services would be in good hands. Fortunately, Theresa had his back when he had to be away. Bennie deeply appreciated his partner-wife. He knew she could carry on very well, facing any problem with a gentle equanimity. Theresa was Bennie's jewel, his coworker and administrator. She was made of tough, resilient fiber! Years later she would write to her daughter Pam, unwittingly revealing the source of her equanimity in every situation:

> You don't have the slightest idea about the 1930s. It would be compared to living in the interior jungle here. Even the interior has more than I ever had. I was born in 1935. We had a windmill on the farm to pump our water that we carried into the house. We carried wood in for the stove. My mom heated a big boiler of water

every Saturday so my two little brothers and I could have a bath in the same water. Our long-john underwear got washed on Monday with a washing machine that had a gas motor. We had kerosene lamps for light, and an icebox for keeping our food cold. My mom made me three dresses out of used printed sugar or flour sacks. There were nine in the family. Dad had a '35 Ford, quite small so only half of us could go to church on a Sunday so we took turns. It was a three-hour drive to church and back. We walked a mile in deep snow to catch a car to a one-room school with all eight grades. Two kids in my first grade class.

We planted most of our food. Our dinner was usually fried potatoes and applesauce from our orchard. We carried a lunch pail to school with a bottle of milk, bread and butter and an apple. We got our spending money picking potatoes and planting green beans until I was 16. And I paid for my piano lessons from that as we always had a piano at home. My dad had a violin. He was a carpenter and drove eight miles to town every day. But I never felt deprived, even though our trail to the woods led to the back outhouse with an old Sears catalog for toilet paper.

Even when we pastored in River-de-Chute, near Perth, our house was the pits. Our bathroom was all snowed in with an ice ring for a sit-down toilet at -30° all during January. No water, but we did have lights. I don't know how I would agree to live in such a place. I know some day I will have a modern house, so that's okay.

Theresa could lead a service, teach, preach, and play her accordion. She was always at the altar to pray long and hard with each of the serious ones who sought God. Some claimed she prayed so hard and danced with them in worship clinging to their hands held high, that they "received their portion in self-defense!"

Within two years of using the floatplane as a tool for evangelization, the DeMerchants' efforts stretched from Maués in the east to Cruzeiro do Sul on the southwest—a giant, river-following curve, a fertile crescent of potential for a great harvest of souls for the kingdom of God.

Cessna 172
UPC seaplane

Floating hangar

Recommissioned 4

Meanwhile, the central Manaus church was experiencing revival. Brothers Spears and Hattabaugh held services for eleven days in early January 1973, and fifteen people, including Beth, received the Holy Ghost. This riled Satan, of course. Outsiders threw several smaller stones and brick pieces, but the praying saints just ignored the rat-a-tat of the rocks on the roof and kept on praying, loudly as they do when seeking for the Holy Ghost. Then the hecklers heaved half a cement block through the aluminum roof. Bennie heard it crash against the metal, looked up, and saw it tear through the thin covering. It plummeted to the floor and smashed between two people, shattering to pieces between the front bench and the platform. Had the block hit the people, they could have been seriously injured, maybe killed.

Bennie left the platform and scooped up some of the jagged pieces. Returning to the microphone, he said, "Here's proof that Satan doesn't want you to receive the Holy Ghost!"

The folks prayed even harder and several received their Pentecostal blessing, even with rocks peppering the roof and opening small holes in it. The rock-throwing stopped the next evening when word got around outside that a Baptist senator was inside in the service (looking for votes, of course).

Up to this time, Bennie had been flying Gilberto north to the Abonari and Alalaú Rivers, but in late January 1974 a call came asking for his help in rescuing an Indian in Pará State east of Manaus. A man had cut his leg while working with a machete and lost a lot of blood. On top of it all, he was very ill from a snakebite. The place was at the upper end of a long, narrow lake.

Bennie planned to spend the night on the lake and return to Manaus in the morning, but he learned that the Indian station was out of medicine and the man was getting worse. When Bennie arrived, the man was practically lifeless. He had lost a lot of blood and his tongue was as white as paper.

Using the lights of Manaus and a white-sand beach about a mile and a half from his homebase, Bennie settled the plane on the water. Three men at the base secured the plane and helped Bennie carry the man out under the strut and up the bank to the Jeep pickup truck. Bennie started for Manaus in the Jeep, but halfway to town the points on the truck froze at a good speed in high gear. It suddenly burst loose, blowing the muffler and tailpipe apart. Bennie could see fire flaring between the Jeep and the pavement before he was able to stop. He ditched the vehicle and hailed a taxi to take the Indian on to the hospital. Though in critical condition, the man did pull through.

Almost before Bennie could catch his breath from that escapade, FUNAI wanted him to fly their doctor to another place where ten Indians had broken out with measles. Flu or even a bad cold often proved fatal to the Indians with their low resistance to such white man's diseases.

As absolutely necessary and indispensable as the floatplane was, Bennie found that the little Cessna 172 couldn't handle the type of loads needed to fly workers out to preaching-teaching points on weekends. Men and their gear plus Bibles, tracts, hammocks, and other supplies overloaded the faithful little plane. The floats were too small and sank down too far to lift a heavily loaded plane from the water. Bigger floats required a bigger engine, a bigger engine needed a bigger airframe, and so forth.

Shortly after Bennie realized he needed a larger plane, he returned to Manaus from a trip to Buenos Aires. He buckled down for a couple of hours in a guest seat in the pilot's cabin and chatted with the captain as he piloted the big aircraft around storms using radar.

Both delighted and astonished by the advanced equipment on the commercial flight, Bennie continued his investigation into the possibility of obtaining a larger plane. Finally he wrote Paul Box:

> Considering the shortness of time [before Bennie and Teresa would be going on furlough], and that said aircraft should be owned by the United Pentecostal Church International some months before being donated to the United Pentecostal Church of Brazil for importing as a donation to avoid import taxes and duty, proper action should be taken at this General Conference, if it is decided that any action will be taken.
>
> I am hereby soliciting an appropriation from SFC (Sheaves for Christ) of $25,000 towards the purchase of a Cessna 185 six-place float plane in the early summer of 1975, if the Lord wills and tarries.

Bennie and Theresa loved their work, frustrating as it sometimes was. No doubt about it; their roots were digging deeper in the Amazon River region. A few workers, trained in the Bible school in Rio de Janeiro, were doing excellent work. Bennie felt, however, that more helpers would be coming soon, and these would be located in the vast, watery spread of jungle villages where the plane would tie them together. A bigger plane could carry workers in and out on various rivers with ease and with no worry of overloading the craft. And there was no dearth of rivers—there were hundreds in the Amazon Basin alone.

Then a huge surprise delighted the DeMerchants. An even bigger plane than Bennie had requested had been ordered! It was not a 185, but a much larger 206 Cessna with a Robertson Short Take Off and Landing (STOL) kit. Colored tropical orange/nutmeg, it sported the brightest combination for being seen on jungle rivers. The DeMerchants were due for a furlough in 1975, and at the end of that time, Bennie would fly the 206 back to Brazil.

Several events marked the DeMerchants' calendar with out-of-the-routine days. A man with his eight-year-old daughter had traveled to Manaus, only to have the little girl be run over by a car. People who live in rural river areas are confused and disoriented by the congested, high-speed traffic of a metropolis. They arrive in the city and do not really check the traffic both ways before crossing a street. With a heavy heart, Bennie flew to the family's home in the interior. Arriving there about 3:00 AM, he awakened the little girl's mother and flew the sobbing, heartbroken woman through the night to her child's funeral. At a time like this, Bennie would have easily given this part of his job to someone else.

During the weeks while the discussion about a larger aircraft was being conducted, FUNAI asked Bennie to fly a doctor and vaccines to treat over 150 Indians on an Indian outpost on the Nhamundá River. To his surprise, he met an Indian fellow there who had walked over the Guiana watershed in about ten days. The man, another evangelical believer, had been to school. He could read and write basic

English. While the doctor vaccinated the Indians, Bennie fished around in the glove compartment of the plane and removed his New Testament. Together, the Indian and the missionary read the second chapter of Acts in English and talked a lot. Again, Bennie wondered if there would ever be a work among the Indian people.

Then at the end of 1974, the murder of Gilberto was splashed across the front of the newspapers. A saddened Bennie remembered the nearly two hundred hours in the 172 with Gilberto, flying far up many Amazon tributaries, sometimes in one week, to carry medicines or medical personnel into probably thirty outposts, splashing down along the way.

Bennie grieved over the last picture taken of Gilberto, his arms around two of the chiefs who the following morning had commanded the attack that killed him and three of his men. Bennie recognized many of the faces in the photo, for he had visited that Indian outpost with Gilberto on several occasions. The Army had found the camera used to take the picture, and had developed the film, and the regional FUNAI supervisor shared the photos with Bennie.

Such trade-offs with the Brazilian government worked to everyone's advantage. When he could, Bennie usually arranged these early in the week. The new road being built from Manaus to Boa Vista BR-174 (Brazilian Roadway 174) entailed a huge amount of labor. The Trans-Amazon Engineering Company needed to find the type of rocks, sand, and clay desired for the road, since the fill over swampy areas had to stand up to heavy winter rains. About 250 miles north of Manaus, the company had a large group of men who had eaten all their food supplies. Rapids roiled the river, the Indian territory that the road traversed had suffered several massacres just the past year, and the road crew needed supplies in a hurry!

In the effort to supply them, Bennie had no competition. The area on the Jauaperi River scared off any other amphibian or floatplane because of the heavy jungle and the rock-filled Alalaú River: No other pilot even wanted to fly anywhere near that Indian reserve! Bennie liked the deal, though, because the money from the flight underwrote the work. The money Bennie earned from this particular contract sent several students to Rio for Bible school, put an aluminum roof on the Maués church, and bought a loudspeaker system for the Eirunepé church. Bennie also squirreled away some money into a savings account for parts, components, or rebuilt engines for the plane. Due to the humidity and high temperatures of the Amazon, engines had short lives.

In April 1975, the DeMerchants began planning their itinerary for travel during their furlough. If it weren't for brief family reunions and the opportunity to thank their many supporters, the DeMerchants would have preferred to stay in Brazil where their work kept them busy, happy, and fulfilled despite the many frustrations and obstacles. No good time existed to take a furlough in the middle of a fast-growing work that also required constant air services. A peek at their proposed furlough itinerary reveals almost constant travel.

After arriving in St. Louis for a debriefing, they planned to visit Theresa's family in Madison, Wisconsin; submit to medical exams in St. Paul; prepare their display for the services they would conduct; drive to Perth, New Brunswick, Canada for reunion with Bennie's family and settling the girls in school; and deputation travel in the Canadian Atlantic districts. September took them to the General Conference in Fort Worth, Texas, and the School of Missions in St. Louis. Bennie spent a couple weeks around Christmas time taking an aviation instrument flight training course. After another twenty hours in a simulator and twenty more with an instrument instructor in the airplane, he received his instrument rating. They returned to deputation travel in the Northeastern mini-districts, circling throughout the eastern US and returning to New Brunswick to be with family until the girls terminated their school term. They waited there until the birth of their third child, a boy they named Bennie Jonas.

At the end of their furlough, the DeMerchants planned for Theresa, Pam, and baby Jonas to return later to Manaus by commercial flight. Bennie with Beth and Clayton Goodine flew the new Cessna 206 back to Brazil. *This new plane will be able to carry nearly twice the load of the smaller 172 Cessna,* Bennie thought. He let his mind wander over the tremendous blessing that would be in ferrying workers, materials, and supplies to the established churches, and how instrumental it would be in reaching even farther across the Amazon Basin in less time than it took in the 172.

Barely three days after returning to Brazil, Bennie answered a call to attend a five-church fellowship rally in Maués. The resulting attempted flight in the new plane ended in disaster to the plane and snuffed out the lives of José Cinque, who had been supervising the work in Eirunepé, and of Missionary Margaret Calhoun. The nightmarish incident in August 1976 shook Bennie to his very core until the Lord appeared to him and told him to get on with the work and that He would bless Bennie and the work as never before.

Immediately after the accident, Bennie thought deeply and seriously about continuing without the plane, but when he got letters from the interior churches describing their problems, he realized flying was the only way to reach the Amazon Basin. When he was preaching among the various churches, he was like the man who couldn't see the forest for the trees, but when he was away, such as on furlough, his mind's eye traveled up and down the Amazon River thinking about the pockets of Jesus Name believers that he would love to see.

One night a few weeks later, Bennie and a couple of workers sneaked into a church right in the middle of the jungle, walking from the truck through the woods to reach the building. He was amazed to see wonderful things going on after his being away fourteen months. A great spirit of worship permeated the church in the much-too-small building. The pastor was doing well and the saints were supporting him.

Thanking the Lord for the progress he saw, Bennie felt renewed and recommissioned. He realized it was time for him to lift the Cessna 172 back into the air and start flying again.

A rural church

A beautiful Amazonian family

More Pies than Appetite

In October after the tragic plane crash, Bennie wrote to S. G. Norris, president of the Apostolic Bible Institute in St. Paul, Minnesota. Brother Norris, a staunch supporter of Bennie and Theresa's work in Brazil, had written an encouraging letter to Bennie after the horrendous, life-taking accident.

Bennie replied, "Elder, I have been running straight since I landed in Brazil. I have my finger in about thirty different pies. I love to be busy, but the pressures from being overly busy make me squirm and I always keep thinking that next month I'll be on top."

Being away on furlough was bad enough; coming back only to have the new plane crash and cause the deaths of two enthusiastic workers was even worse. The mountain of work looming over him seemed insurmountable. Then he listed the things that needed immediate attention—and some of the items that distracted him:

1. Accident from plane and side effects. Official translator, 10 trips;
2. Absence of wife and having to take care of Beth's schooling;

3. Get a vehicle in shape that had about fifteen things to be done to it;

4. Attend city church meetings and defuse problems in interior churches;

5. Update tax filing. (Two days earlier he had received a notice from Brazil's IRS equivalent to the effect that their CGC, a general Federal number for tax purposes that must be presented for any sale or purchase, needed to be updated; reporting for '74 and '75 had not been received yet and they would be cancelled . . . and without a CGC his church organization did not exist. The accountant responsible didn't get it done for '74 before they left, so the DeMerchants would be seeing the chief for an extension of twenty days to put their income files in order.);

6. See to financing for new Ford 350 truck from the bank;

7. Restock fuel for rural areas for old floatplane—an absolute necessity;

8. Get documents in order for motor vehicle inspection, radio insurance, etc;

9. Completely replace all electrical component wires from engine firewall forward due to the fire the mission had while they were away;

10. Replace windshield. Theresa would bring it with her and would have to pay 250 percent duty on it;

11. Install new spray flanges with riveter to protect the propeller on old plane;

12. Replace rusted exhaust couplers and a multitude of other maintenance replacements;

13. Remove old engine from crashed plane and crate it for shipment to US after accident inspectors released it. Remove the wings and struts and put

them overhead in the hangar and pull the crashed plane fuselage and floats inside;

14. Build two extra rooms in hangar for storing the parts from the 206;

15. Repair two outboard motors;

16. Tow the hangar into the main Rio Negro because the cove was going dry for lack of rain;

17. Erect aluminum pavilion for a spring crusade on new lot bought in Compensa;

18. Oil seal worked loose on new truck. It will take the car dealer's maintenance shop a week to take care of that and some minor things that are included in the guarantee;

19. Assemble materials for making fifty more benches for Castelo Branco;

20. Re-dig the church cesspool very soon; will need to separate soapy water from other materials;

21. Re-roof Castelo Branco church, the house behind it, the mission house in Ramos Ferreira, Margaret's apartment, and the garage behind it before the rainy season hits;

22. The interior brethren were begging him to come. Jonas had a big thing planned in Maués for the fifteenth of the following month. Bennie was to be in the Eirunepé area on the first for a few days. Straighten out motor problem on Marrecão Island;

23. Build an extension on the Santo Antonio church near Manacapuru. It's too small, has a low ceiling, and gets very hot;

24. Must change the frequency in the house radio and put up a couple new, higher-reaching antennas;

25. Help Jonas in building a new church near Parintins;

26. Tow the floating church into a lake ten miles away where house meetings are going well. Ozeca, a worker, is encouraged to see some results;

27. Completely overhaul little plane's engine;
28. Replace the Coroado house they tore down;
29. Try to get at least one telephone in the house for Pelejandro: hope that after three years the request will go through;
30. Go to Rio and be with Robert Norris for a few days of preaching, teaching, talking, and encouraging him in the Lord. He's got 130 things to do;
32. Build in three places at about the same time.

Just thinking about all the things on the list made Bennie shudder. Thankfully, he reported that the churches were in fairly good shape. Even with all the problems, both DeMerchants felt that Manaus was their home and worried all the time they were away.

"Last year on furlough was the longest year of my life," Bennie finished his letter. "Brother Scism wrote last month of the possibility of my looking at 'greener fields' and being tempted to take a pastorate in the States. Pray tell me, where could one have a more challenging life than on the mission field?"

Meeting the Indians

The personnel of FUNAI contracted with Bennie to fly them to Indian outposts, one at Nhamundá and the others on the Alalaú River. The government officials had negotiated with some Wai-Wai Indians from Guiana to mediate between the fierce Atroaris and FUNAI. The Wai-Wais spoke some English, Portuguese, and shared much of the Atroaris language.

"I met six Wai-Wai Indians from British Guiana who speak English," Bennie wrote his friend Gerald Grant. "They are believers from a Baptist mission and have their own Bible. They pray before meals. It's funny to see them with their ornamental feathers and lack of dress. However, they do wear a type of Bermuda shorts. They speak their own language and some of the language of the Atroaris."

The Indians had trekked south about fifteen days from Guiana to Nhamundá with the Hiscariano Indians. One day while there with the chief of FUNAI, Bennie learned from the Wai-Wai chief that they had converted the Hiscarianos. They had learned about the Bible while in Guiana. Curious, Bennie entered their church. It was about sixty feet in diameter, over forty feet high—with a shape like a clown's hat—and covered with thatch. The

Indians asked Bennie about his work and what he did with the plane. Bennie explained he had works and churches all along the river. He also told them about the broken leg he had had a year earlier. Two or three of them had seen a car, so they explained to the others how Bennie had been injured in the city. As he talked about the Holy Ghost, others sauntered over. About 150 Indians gathered around and they wanted to see where his leg was broken and fixed. Obligingly, Bennie showed them the scar on his shin and the collarbone that stuck out.

The chief of FUNAI didn't speak English, so he didn't know what was going on. He wanted to take a picture of the Indians but they had left him and had wandered over to where Bennie sat. He politely accused Bennie of trying to teach them religion, but Bennie replied he was only talking to them about the plane and showing them the scar from an accident. The FUNAI chief accepted this and let it go at that. Bennie smiled to himself at these Wai-Wais who had migrated south from Guiana. In the Indians' language, which none of the government people spoke beyond a vocabulary of about fifty words, these Indians had done more in a year than a mission society could do in ten. When FUNAI's Volkswagen van brought their chief of the Wai-Wais to Manaus, they would allow him to visit the DeMerchants' home where Bennie hoped to have a good talk with him.

The Atroaris were filtering back to the outposts even though the road to Boa Vista had been completed. All of these outposts had HF SSB radios that were on the same frequency and so it was like a huge party line. The radio man in FUNAI headquarters in Manaus could call outpost by outpost by name, and they would respond twice a day in early morning and late afternoon. They reported health status and other information of interest, including any movement of any outsider or visitors and their motor canoes. At these border areas, the outposts were the eyes and ears of the government and valuable for combating drug or miner interlopers. Outsiders liked to slip into the foothills in the jungle and prospect for gold or other things, and tried to bypass the Indians. The Indians could always see the scraped-off scar of a canoe if someone pushed it over a slime-laden log underwater in a creek. They also could note where the passing of a human or animal on a jungle trail broke a green twig and left the foot or paw print embedded into damp leaves collected on the jungle floor. The Indians' food depended on their hunting and tracking skills in the jungle.

After Christmas 1976, Bennie had a week of keeping home fires burning in the local city churches. The brief interlude of rest felt so good! Then FUNAI sent a reporter and photographer from one of Brazil's largest newspapers to Bennie to fly the men over the Indians to get some shots of the Waimiris.

"The reporter had gone with an air taxi and spent a lot of money, but they didn't know where the Indians were located," Bennie wrote to Gerald. "I guaranteed him before takeoff that he would see Indians or I would pay for the flight. The first Indian communal house produced about thirty-five Indians running around naked in a clearing below."

Before the Atroaris killed Gilberto, Bennie had mentally marked the clearings with the silhouettes of the hills in the jungle as cross-fixes. For example, going south from an axe-head turn in the river for five minutes or 90 degrees from an inlet for ten minutes at three thousand feet altitude put him within sight of a large hut in a clearing. While the reporter and photographer positioned their long-snouted telescopic camera, Bennie could tell them how many seconds they were away from a clearing. With tall cypress trees poking above the green jungle, he spotted their trunks from its opposite side. He said nothing, dropped down, and headed in that direction. When at about the exact moment he had predicted the clearing appeared, the disbelieving photographer shook his head in surprise. Bennie chuckled inwardly at their amazement. He wouldn't be paying for this flight, but they would be!

Aerial view of Indian village

A Handy Andy, Please

Early one morning Bennie was giving Theresa a verbal list of all he had to do.

"What do you need to do first?" Theresa asked.

"Everything," Bennie answered. "Everything should be at the top of the list under 'priorities.' But I can do only one thing at a time. While I am doing one chore, three more things pop up."

Bennie had gotten to the point that when he saw "Rev." written on a letter in front of his name, he began to think it must be because he kept revved up most of the time. Obviously, he needed a helper. But just not any old helper would do.

"I need a man or a couple who know the difference between a slot and a Phillips screwdriver," Bennie continued. "I get bogged down with just run-of-the mill affairs. I need someone who can adapt to either a Howard Johnson's or a hammock between the trees. The helper must be able to adjust to our hot, humid climate. He should be able to take over a construction project with workers and converse with them in Portuguese and tell everyone else what to do. I need a rough carpenter, a bricklayer, an electrician, a plumber, an automobile and airplane mechanic, a truck driver, and a person who can eventually turn into a teacher and preacher of the Word all rolled into one. He should be able to learn Portuguese conversationally in a year and technically in two years if he goes into the ministry. I need to find all this in one man. As time goes on, he would probably become a regular missionary and move into a new area."

Bennie had been depending on national workers, but though hard working, they were limited in the range of their abilities. A national who could lay bricks might not be able to do mechanical work, carpentry, or drive a truck. Brother and Sister Robert Norris, missionaries in Rio de Janeiro, operated a Bible school there, and several of their students after graduation returned to the Manaus area. It was a win-win situation for Bennie because he often had young people wanting to go to Bible school for training. However, Bennie had a different kind of worker in mind.

"I see a lot of projects looming next year and I need a Handy Andy who I can show the project to and he could pick it up and go on from there," Bennie explained.

Then the Indian Department asked Bennie to fly a doctor to the Indians on the Nhamundá River. The Indians there had broken out with fever and dysentery. One elderly lady was in a coma. The doctor took in a pile of equipment and needed to spend the night, so Bennie had to stay overnight too. While at supper, Bennie ate a couple of fresh Brazil nuts and mentioned that he liked them. An Indian who understood a few words of Portuguese tugged on Bennie's shirt and asked to trade his Brazil nuts for Bennie's shirt.

"I only have one shirt," Bennie explained, denying the Indian's request.

"Manaus has more," the Indian replied.

When Bennie rolled out of his hammock the next morning, the Indian stood there with half a pail of shelled nuts, still wanting Bennie's shirt. The Indian had gone out earlier, climbed a Brazil nut tree, picked the nuts, and shelled them.

The doctor laughed. "You opened your mouth about liking the nuts so he went out and got them. You have to come across or they'll all be mad."

Bennie handed over his shirt and retreated to the plane to escape the sun. The doctor, still laughing about Bennie's loss, grabbed Bennie's camera and took a picture of him without a shirt on but holding two bags of Brazil nuts, standing beside the Indian who was just buttoning up the shirt.

Shortly afterward, FUNAI tagged Bennie again to help resolve some problems. So he airlifted the agent and four Federal police into the reserve to seize six men who had infiltrated the area, hunting illegally within one mile of where Gilberto was killed. These poachers may have been taking potshots at the Indians, causing them to distrust anyone working with the government. The hunters had sneaked up the river at night in canoes, but three of the men from FUNAI discovered their food and ammunition cache, took their guns, hid them, and let the hunters come back for the night. When the hunters came back after dark, they were caught by surprise, apprehended, and brought back to the Comanaú outpost. The FUNAI men radioed Manaus, held an inquiry, and processed the men— and Bennie was in for a job!

Later that week Bennie took Manoel, his assistant in Manaus, and Jonas and their wives to Parintins. Among their baggage were eighty injections, some groceries, and three bottles of liquid stove gas that weighed sixty pounds apiece. They stopped at the Hiscariano Indian tribe. It was prohibited to go there without permission, but on the last trip the department had forgotten to buy the needed items. This tribe would only be about forty-five minutes off course so Bennie decided to take these items to the

Indians. Believers in some form of Baptist doctrine were right in the middle of the round, thatch-roofed church teaching the Indians choruses in Portuguese. Bennie had forgotten to tell them beforehand that FUNAI didn't allow any religious work among them by outsiders.

"One day when they do open this area up," Bennie wrote to Gerald, "I hope we can be ready to step in."

A week later, Bennie traveled to a new place 250 miles east where their worker Jonas had been visiting with a boat. It was getting dark and Bennie's long legs did not want to lose any time. The men strode quickly through a narrow path in the high grass along the river, listening to people singing in the thatch-roofed house in the distance. Suddenly Bennie nearly trod on a poisonous snake. He froze a second, then leaped backward, screaming, "Cobra!"

The people behind him stopped just as quickly. The cobra slithered off into the grass. If it had struck Bennie in his bare sandals, he would have been spitting blood in a few minutes. He had seen men die quickly after a cobra bite.

"I know Jesus gave us power to tread on serpents," he declared, "but I would rather keep my distance."

Soon the men arrived at the new meetinghouse. It had a mud floor and strong roof and walls with a little room behind it. To provide seats, the worshipers had put boards across some stumps. The house was packed inside and out, so Bennie slipped around to the back room to get in. When it was time for the altar call, the people were jammed in too tightly to move, so Bennie had them come around outside to the side window. Jonas and Bennie stretched their arms outside the open window and prayed with people. Nine souls came to the Lord for the first time. Afterward they walked to the river and baptized fifteen in Jesus' name. Bennie didn't know where the snake went but though he stayed alert for it, he didn't see the creature again.

Bennie's next flight took him and Manoel seven hundred miles west to the Eirú River. There they baptized eight people. One old man owned an entire 100-mile length of the river. His several sons administered a large rubber plantation. Bennie's heart yearned over the people who lived and worked there. The workers accepted the owner as their material father and sold their rubber balls of latex to him at his price. They bought their foodstuffs at his store in the jungle at his price and never got out of debt. They would work all their life and die owing him money according to his records.

The people living there were cut off from the outside world. Due to fog, Bennie had to land the plane in front of the house of one of the rich man's sons. This son was very sick, so later in the morning Bennie took him in the plane to get emergency medical treatment. He later claimed Bennie saved his life. This opened up the whole river to the gospel and soon there were twenty-seven believers beyond his house. The worker went up there for services traveling two days in a canoe with a motor.

Then wonder of wonders happened back in Manaus. After being on the waiting list for four years, the DeMerchants got a telephone in their house. What an advantage having the telephone in house was! No more running to town in the car for messages. They hardly had a chance to get used to such a luxury when the Interior Department chief of FUNAI phoned, wanting Bennie to go to an Indian outpost to get a sick woman and her husband. He took off at 6:30 PM and flew 120 miles. After getting the couple into a FUNAI ambulance, he loaded three hundred pounds of cargo and took off. On the return, he was to pick up a doctor he'd left at Nhamundá the previous week. But fifteen minutes out, Theresa radioed Bennie to tell him that the interior ministry chief had another sick case in Rio Andirá who needed to be taken to Parintins to the hospital before Bennie could go on to Nhamundá.

After confirming the messages, Bennie changed course again. He would need to stop in Maués to get fuel at the church there. In the meantime he would get to see Pastor Jonas and a worker in Parintins where he intended to spend the night. The next day he began another seven-hour run up the Purús River to Lábrea, but the $800 a day he was earning would bolster the in-the-red building fund.

Flying wasn't the only thing occupying Bennie's time. He was currently helping to build one small church on the Trans-Amazon highway about two hours north from Manaus where a worker had a good group of believers. Bennie gave him some bags of cement and aluminum for the roof of the building. The people there would have to get the rest.

The mission was still plodding along on the new lot addition in Coronado, which was not walled in. They were laying the foundation for walls of another dormitory for interior people who would come to their state convention at the end of October. Bennie was also working away slowly on the Compensa church and a structure for a larger, open-sided place where they could get one thousand people seated. On the opposite side of the river from Manacapuru where the Amazon was about four miles wide, they planned to build a small church and another one in Manacari soon.

In this whirlwind of activity, Bennie wrote Gerald,

> What I fear may be forced on me. The work will grow to a point that I can't keep up in visiting and teaching in all the places and will probably have to start a part-time Bible school at least for the married couples who will not be able to

go to Rio. This requires a lot of organization, supervision, help, and just plain work, but it looks like that time is coming closer. I have about six or seven going to Rio, but we do have some problems. Those from the north of Brazil experience a different culture than those from the south; some of the students marry; a few are sent home; they have different levels of education; and only about 50 percent go into the ministry. Those who do go into the ministry usually succeed in doing a good work for God. For the time being, however, the only way to be truly effective is to get the workers and pastors and have them come in for 15 days every so often to teach them here in Manaus.

In spite of the incredible workload, Bennie would sometimes take the time to be just a dad. Both girls loved to fish, and one time they had a contest going. The lake, though low, was full of bass, and many times both Beth and Pam hooked fish at the same time. Bennie changed flies, clubbed fish, and kept score. Beth caught twenty-four, Pam hooked twenty, and Bennie managed to snag eleven. They bagged seventy-five pounds of fish! Theresa feared the girls would become tomboys, but Bennie preferred that to their going shopping and spending money. Besides, the dog, Pastor, ate fish too, so that meant less dog food for them to buy.

Halfway through the year, Leo Upton arrived to hold services throughout the Amazon. Bennie loved the elderly evangelist and was amazed by his stamina. In seven or eight nights in six different places, seventy-six received the Holy Ghost and thirty-three were baptized in Jesus' name.

"There is great joy in the churches," Bennie reported to Gerald. "I would hardly believe it had I not seen it. Brother Upton goes slow and makes it so simple. He talks about repenting, then how to believe that the Lord will keep His word, then how to concentrate on Jesus and not be distracted by other thoughts. He tells them to praise the Lord and receive the Holy Ghost by faith and not to be afraid when they start to speak in another language."

Waves of glory rolled over a congregation when everyone was involved in one super-huge altar call. The ones who received the Holy Ghost would immediately afterward help the others. Bennie saw chronic seekers who would hardly whisper praise break out and receive a marvelous experience that lasted after the service because they were so drunk on the Spirit they couldn't return to Portuguese! By the time Bennie put Brother Upton on the plane to Rio, 141 Brazilians had received the Holy Ghost in twenty-five days.

"These people have been bringing other folks into our church off the street," Bennie added. "I baptized a preacher whose relative received the Holy Ghost in our church two or three months ago. The preacher has a group of about 75 believers on the Rio Negro an hour and a half flying time from here. They have not received the Holy Ghost and he wants us to go up there and baptize them in Jesus' name and pray them through. We have no works on this river yet so this may open up a new area for me, but I don't know how I will be able to take care of all that's going on."

Before the end of the year, however, Bennie received a letter from Gerald recommending a good, all-around young man named John Bono. Then he got a letter from the young man himself. In answering, Bennie outlined exactly what kind of help he needed. His tough, rough letter barred no holds.

It didn't dissuade John. Even with Bennie's put-it-to-him letter, he wanted to help in the Amazon.

Then competition developed between the church in Parintins and a local church of a different denomination. The pastor in Parintins had developed a nice congregation and Bennie went to dedicate their church. Earlier they had bought a corner lot for a church in town and the local church had bought a lot on the opposite corner. When the UPCB started to build, the local church did also. When the people ran out of cash and stopped building, so did the other group. Finally the UPCB built the sides and the roof.

"We had the dedication service for our church and the church across the street decided to have their dedication the same day without walls on their building," Bennie wrote Gerald. "Well, we had a happy time and the church was full. The church with no walls across the street could hear us preaching and we preached for them to hear! We started praying and one man miraculously got the baptism of the Holy Ghost. They quit their service and many of that congregation walked over to see something they hadn't seen. In the evening service that night, some of them were in our service. End of competition!"

Other groups were breaking away from nonbiblical doctrines and were being baptized in Jesus' name by the dozens, including their preachers. In northern Brazil between 350 and 400 were baptized in Jesus' name that year and in the last half of the year over 225 people received the baptism of the Holy Ghost. The DeMerchants were swamped with responsibility and work.

Where, oh where, was that Handy Andy?

Pamela loves riding horses.

Leo Upton roughing it for Jesus

The Holy Ghost Trail

A Volkswagen taxi rammed the back of the "ole green rocket" pickup truck Theresa was driving, smashing in the Bug. A furious taxi driver jumped from his car and yelled at Theresa, demanding she pay up on the spot.

"I'm not responsible," she answered calmly. "You are. You ran into the back of my truck."

The cabdriver was livid. Grabbing a wheel wrench, he circled around to the front of the truck and smashed out both headlights with the tool. Then he coolly got in the Volkswagen and drove off.

Theresa laughed at his ridiculous behavior. A crowd gathered and pitied her. An evangelical among the watchers felt so sorry for her that he told her the Lord would pay her back. Not missing an opportunity to possibly win the man to the Lord, she quickly handed him some Oneness literature and invited him to the upcoming campaign. He promised to come.

When she got home Bennie grinned at her story. "I was going to change both sealed beam lights for the inspection in March anyway," he told her. "The low beam on one is burned out and the high beam on the other side is too. When I switch beams at night it looks like the old green pickup is winking. Rather than get a fine I'll just drive with the parking lights and use the sealed beams out in areas where there are streetlights. Seems every time the devil lifts his foot to kick us, he bites his own toes."

Bennie had preached that "everything that can be shaken will be. Don't aggrandize your problems but minimize them to their right size because the devil wants to put everyone on the run over nothing."

Before long, Bennie had an opportunity to prove his own counsel. He scraped the paint on a woman's car when parking and she almost grabbed him by the neck, thinking he was trying to sneak off without claiming responsibility.

"Now, ma'am," he calmed her, "you can see this street is very narrow and full of traffic. I'm sorry. I was in a hurry and two drivers were blowing their horns behind me, so I scooted in here and scraped the paint off your fender. I'm a pastor, at fault. Have the scraped place fixed and send me the bill."

Bennie gave her his address, smiled, and strolled over to the bank, dumbfounding the Brazilians. They would rather fight and argue at who is to fault until at times one person kills the other. In the church Bennie tried to get to the bottom of things and simplify the problem. He would ask the people what they ought to do . . . and encourage them to follow through on their solution.

Problems arose, but some of them turned out to be wonderfully happy ones. One Sunday night in the central church, the saints held an hour-long prayer meeting during which four received the Holy Ghost in the prayer room. When service time came at seven, Bennie tried to get the people who were praying to join the service in the auditorium. Outsiders were entering the auditorium, and Bennie wanted those in the prayer room to hear the evangelist. He spent half an hour trying to get them to stop. Some couldn't stop praying in tongues and about ten of them were just plain drunk on the Spirit as on the Day of Pentecost. Bennie stood in the door and would persuade one to go into the auditorium, but when he turned his back to get another pray-er, the first one would sneak back in to pray some more.

With Brazilians praying like that, is it any surprise that a new work was being initiated in Parintins, a city of about sixty thousand people? A church in Parintins would stretch Bennie's flying range eighty-five more miles to the east. With the opening of this new work, churches would ring Manaus in every direction like points on a compass.

In northern Brazil between 350 and 400 folks had been baptized in Jesus' name that year and in the last half of the year over 225 people received the baptism of the Holy Ghost. They also were having a good revival with a young minister and his wife who had been rebaptized and then joined them. This young minister had been preaching in Coroado, a suburb area northeast of downtown Manaus where Theresa and her maid started a work by home visits with tracts. During the revival, they had to take the pews out of the church for the people to get inside. A number were healed and about thirty baptized in water. The harvest started to come in.

The DeMerchants had never seen anything like this before. One morning after Sunday school, Bennie baptized twenty-three folks. It was Carnival time, but the DeMerchants' answer for that was to have morning services from nine o'clock to twelve o'clock in the central church for the new converts. It made Bennie cry within to see a church packed out with everyone seeking the Lord and waves of glory rolling through the congregation with the people shouting, weeping, and praising the Lord.

Satan wasn't very happy about this. Bennie flew the plane to Belém where a man who pastored five small Oneness churches was quite discouraged. Part of his problem was he was not really preaching that people needed to receive the Holy Ghost. Of course he was getting no results in his churches. Bennie encouraged him to preach the Holy Ghost and left the man quite inspired.

The devil continued fighting the DeMerchants tooth and nail. Bennie had gone to Belém on a flight plan. Belém air control authorized him to land on the river close by. Floatplanes were not a usual sight in Belém, and someone, seeing suitcases, assumed they were full of contraband and reported him to the authorities. The authorities, thinking the plane was loaded with hash, seized the plane while Bennie was in a church service. Bennie had forgotten to put the overflight permit in the window and left just a telephone number at the yacht club. The next morning when he reached the plane, eight armed naval marines were under orders to let no one in or near the plane.

The United States Consulate, the Brazilian admiral of the Navy, the Port Authority, and the FBI of Brazil had been sweeping Belém looking for Bennie while he was sleeping in a hammock after a late evening church service. The Center of Aeronautics had not advised the other authorities. They had a fine lined up for him to pay, but Bennie unfolded the M-27 ONC chart and showed them the seaplane base symbol in front of the city of Belém. He explained that he had landed in an approved area. He spent all that day going to each department of the various authorities, waiting to see the right man to present the legal airplane documents of entry and his permanent resident visa card. All was in order. It was quite an experience, and the Brazilian marines guarded the plane well for free. When Bennie got clearance to move, the soldiers had just been ordered to leave.

Happenings that month included:
- A young girl who knew only Portuguese received the Holy Ghost, praising the Lord in perfect American English;

- A lady who couldn't stand up or walk was healed and was now walking to church in Manaus;
- A witch doctor who used to cut herself to offer her blood to evil powers was delivered, baptized, and filled with the Holy Ghost;
- Teenagers who had run away from home and had not contacted their parents in months showed up that very same week;
- One man had had an expensive chainsaw stolen from his house over a month earlier. This particular saw belonged to the company the man worked for, and he was responsible to reimburse its price. He came to church and asked the church to pray that the Lord would help resolve the problem. So they prayed. When the man opened his back door the next morning, there was the power saw on the steps! The poor fellow probably never had been in a Pentecostal church like that and he sure advertised it.

From Belém in the east to Cruzeiro do Sul and on to Rio Branco in Acre State is about two thousand miles. In 1969, Bennie spent what he thought was a wasted afternoon in talking to a young man. Later this young man moved to Rio Branco and in just nine months baptized 640 people in Jesus' name in that city. Bennie preached on Jose Soares's radio program. Between the two places, 1,500 people had been baptized in Jesus' name. What a trail of Spirit-filled believers!

"We cannot let them go like a wild horse," Bennie remarked, "but what can we do to keep up? The bureaucratic bungling, constructing places to worship, pastoring a church, overseeing a district, visiting churches in a state twenty-two times the size of New Brunswick or 5 percent larger than Alaska, keeping an airplane in shape, and trying to live a family life—all keep me at the grindstone." Yet in spite of all the work, Bennie was planning an evangelistic campaign in a suburban area of Manaus where over thirty thousand very poor people lived without running water or electricity.

Bennie often wondered how anything ever got done in Brazil. He went four times to get the old pickup truck inspected and licensed. The inspector said the paint on the fender didn't match the paint on the hood and so the truck could not pass inspection. (In Brazil a person couldn't change the paint color of a vehicle without a permit from the transit department.) So Bennie got another type of green paint a little closer in hue and repainted the fender. Then he sent Theresa to get it okayed. A different man was doing the inspecting. Theresa just smiled at him, and he passed the truck through. Bennie never could figure out what the paint job had to do with car safety.

During this time, Bennie also spent a lot of time in the air. One Tuesday Bennie flew to Beruri, at the mouth of the Purús River, to drop off a fellow working for the Indian Foundation. Wednesday he flew two engineers to the Pará border on the Andirá River. Thursday he flew a doctor and two helpers to São Gabriel da Cachoeira with medicines needed to combat a type of flu, and landed at Comanaú outpost after dark.

He would be up in the air much of the following week as well. On Monday he planned to go east to Autazes, Andirá, Coatá, and Nhamundá for FUNAI. Wednesday his schedule would take him north up the Japurá River almost to the Colombian border to do a flight for a pilot who was in the hospital. An aviation radio inspector from Rio would be going with Bennie to check out the radio stations at the outpost of the Mucú Indians. From there they would hop north of the equator to the mouth of the Içana River, which flows into the Negro River, and return the following day. Then on Friday he was to go up to Barcelos and follow the Aracá River an hour and a half north to a waterfall to leave two men who had people working there among the Indians. To finish out that week he was to take six people arriving from France to the Mamorie River area south of Manaus. Such flights for the Brazilian government procured much-needed funds that would help pay for his upcoming sixteen-hour round-trip to Eirunepé to tend to church business.

Three weeks later Bennie and a worker flew eight hundred miles upriver to Eirunepé. He landed the plane at a place where they planned to hang their hammocks and spend the night. Of course, Bennie hoped to take a few minutes to catch a bass for supper. When he pulled the control to the mixture cable to stop the plane, the cable came out. He slipped down with his feet in the water and then slid across the front spreader bar and poked his head up inside. He took some spinning line and tied the lever in such a way that it would function. However, the mixture haywired into the "rich" position. Later, Bennie and his passenger got home without any trouble, but he did burn ten gallons of gas more than what would have been necessary!

After finishing the repair, Bennie threw a lure into the water from the top of the wing above the windshield. Thirty minutes later he still hadn't snagged a fish. Upon taxiing for takeoff, he thought he saw a patch of grass in the water just ahead in the twilight, but when he neared it, the "grass" made a big splash and disappeared. It was a huge alligator! Remembering his feet had been in the water as he sat on the spreader bar to do the needed repair, Bennie decided that the next time he would paddle the plane to the riverbank and fix it there.

When Bennie arrived back in Manaus, he learned that the Youth and Missions Departments were interested in producing a film for promotional purposes that churches could order. Vince Kelley from California was trying to schedule time with him to film a 16 mm sound movie of the work in the interior in various churches. Brother Kelley had a commercial license with an instrument rating and owned a Cessna 182. He had already done a film on Ecuador. The film would be narrated, and Bennie wondered if showing the film could be substituted for furlough time.

Maybe I can request that every viewing of this film be exchanged for one Partner in Missions for every place the film is shown. Then we wouldn't need a furlough, Bennie mused.

Bennie was also aware that the Indians were being absorbed slowly into civilization and some of those involved in the death of Gilberto had moved under the Indian Foundation's oversight to the edge of the Trans–Amazon highway and had been there six months. Some were learning Portuguese. The outpost chief asked Bennie about the possibility of his teaching them before the Indians got into the amoral life and influence of Manaus. It was unofficial but Bennie hoped to work something out.

In addition, the whole tribe of Hiscarianos (who are westernized but isolated) were Baptist converts. Bennie hoped that when the Indians visited Manaus they would be able to convert some of them into true apostolics, using their intelligent young men and transplanting them back into the tribe. Bennie had standing permission to go into their Nhamundá River outpost at any time on any flight as long as he took one of the Department's men and a few supplies in the extra space in the plane.

Then Theresa had a serious car accident when a Jeep Rural, driven by a sixty-nine-year-old man, charged through a changing light too late and hit the front of the two-year-old Volkswagen. The man's vehicle swerved after hitting her and stopped upside down on the grassy median of the boulevard. Gasoline was running out of the

Rural. Theresa dashed out of her Volkswagen and pulled the elderly Portuguese man out of the Jeep. A can of paint in the car rolled onto Theresa's foot, cutting through her shoe and bruising her foot. She and Pamela were unhurt, but Theresa was very sore and unable to walk the next day.

Bennie estimated the damage to the Bug would be $500. *There must be another revival or something good ahead with this kind of thing happening*, Bennie thought.

Something good was ahead, but it was a some*one* instead of a some*thing*. John Bono, a crackerjack mechanic and recent graduate from ABI in St. Paul, Minnesota, had arrived as an auxiliary missionary. To add blessing to blessing, John was a pilot. Even though his name wasn't Andy—as in Handy Andy—the sorely needed help had come at last.

Baptism is a result of believers hearing the Word.

Thousands have received their baptism
of the Holy Ghost in the Amazon.

Holding a Tiger by Its Tail

"John Bono is here with me now and has been seeing the funny side of things. He is studying Portuguese in the morning, and we are hoping to get another teacher for him. So far so good," Bennie wrote his friend. "We need to put an ad in the paper for a young, attractive single Portuguese teacher. John believes that when he steps on a spot, everything there goes haywire. Well, welcome to Manaus."

Between takeoffs and landings from the left seat of the 172 en route to a bass-fishing hole, John studied Portuguese. If his curly brown head got too hot he dunked it in the pool at the back of the house . . . but that happened between the times he was working on the vehicles or the cowling-less 172 when it broke or needed a part. The knife Gerald sent him was one of his major tools. He claimed he could do an overhaul with it since it had so many components on it.

Bennie and a worker had planned a gospel crusade in Parintins to gather in new people from a barrio full of shacks. A brush arbor possessing electricity and seats for approximately four hundred people had already been built. Vince Kelley, who had come to make the film, accompanied Bennie. The evangelist cast the devil out of fifteen people in the first and second nights of the crusade. This angered the spiritualist leader (Macumbeiro) and when prayer time arrived, he mingled with the people and would not let some of them go forward to be prayed for. Brother Kelley filmed much of this. If spiritualists could have gotten the camera, they would have torn it up. One of them was so mad he took a keychain, stuck it in his mouth, and chewed on the keys. Brother Kelley held on to the camera and zoomed right in on him.

In spite of everyone—local churches, Roman Catholics, spiritualists—turning against the crusade, the Lord healed more than one hundred people of hernias, hearing problems, blindness, deafness, and dumbness. One woman approached Bennie in tears. She had no Bible and wanted Bennie to sell her his. Bennie told her that he used his Bible to preach from but assured her that he would buy some Bibles in Manaus and on the next trip to Parintins would bring the Bibles with him. The campaign brought in eighty to a hundred people, and they would soon need a place in which to worship.

John had gotten tired of constantly studying Portuguese, so Bennie gave him a break and flew with him over to Parintins. Unfortunately, John became quite sick with amoebic dysentery. The sickness laid him up for a week. After a brief recovery, he was invaded by giardia worms. Finally he was able to resume his language study. Some of his natural humor broke through in a letter he wrote to Gerald: "The winter seems to have gone by very fast for me. The weather here has been nice, cool, and rainy. All of these Brazilians catch colds when the temperature drops below 75 degrees! They tell me that summer will be hard and hot though, so I guess it's choose your own poison."

Bennie and Theresa had both attended the convention in São Paulo while the maid stayed behind with the kids. Without any input from Bennie, the conference added five more states to Bennie's responsibility: Roraima, Acre, Rondônia, Pará, and Amapá. This concerned Bennie a great deal. He felt it would be impossible to take care of these new states because of his PIM deficits, which he would have to make up in his furlough in 1980. To his dismay, two missionary families were leaving Brazil, and another was leaving shortly for furlough.

To further John's knowledge of the missionary work, Bennie included him on a five-day trip to Eirunepé. Later, John shared his observations of the trip in a letter to Eleanor Grant:

> We have our farthest church in Eirunepé, about 750 miles from Manaus. The first and most important stop was the one we made at the grocery store on the way to the plane. Bennie came back with a huge box filled with about one hundred eggs, six dozen tomatoes, a few rounds of cheese, and five boxes of caramel candy. When I asked him what it all was for he said, "the restaurant doesn't usually have food." I was afraid to ask any more questions.
>
> Got to the hangar and fired up old Betsy. Yours truly, the handsome young, fearless pilot was going to challenge the unknown of the Amazon wilderness. Bennie said he thought it would be a good time to catch up on his sleep. So I plowed through the skies while Bennie snoozed, caught up on Reader's Digests, and ate caramel candy. "Hey, John, look how nice the candy box fits in the hole where the radio used to be." Bennie carefully checked the compass once in a while as I zig-zagged along, trying to follow some map printed in the 1940s.

Two boxes of caramel candy and seven hours later, we arrived over the city. We circled once, and then he said, "Okay, John, put 'er in over there."

ZOOM! SWOOSH! Boy, we were really sinking fast; the candy must've added the extra weight! I had the nose up and the engine full throttle as I eased the control yoke carefully back into my lap. Finally that wonderful sound came, PLOP! SPLASH! Whew, I had done it again—I had defied gravity. I asked Bennie to lighten up on the candy next time.

We tied up and got out, and then he started to tell me of the "other than desirable conditions" of our living quarters for the weekend. But we were spared when we bumped into a fellow who had built a brand-new "hotel" in the city recently. Of course we had to bribe him a little with a few dozen eggs and a box of you know what . . .

After they returned to Manaus, the central church had a "palm frolic" on Palm Sunday. The young people and some of the older ladies opened palm branches by hand while the men nailed them to the overhead structure of a brush arbor, making a roof for it. That same week John taught the Bible study and Theresa interpreted for him. John still had some type of parasite and hadn't been too well. He had taken three or four different kinds of medicine, but the lab reports still came back positive. Theresa reported that he had no problem with pronunciation, but he was struggling with verb tenses. Easy to get along with, John enjoyed talking with people and was making progress in using Portuguese.

Even though tropical diseases plagued John, he made some keen observations about Brazil. Once John thought they needed a new tire because the old tube had seven patches, but they couldn't find a tube.

"I guess that's not bad for around here," John noted. "I saw a guy put the eighteenth patch on a skinny motorcycle tube the other day."

John admitted that his digestive system didn't seem to want to get in the groove there in Brazil. He'd been put on a very restricted diet. He sent his eating schedule for the week to Gerald:

> Monday, gruel with water;
> Tuesday, water with gruel;
> Wednesday, gruel with water;
> Thursday, water and gruel;
> Friday, gruel without water;
> Saturday, water with gruel;
> But on Sunday, it's a special treat!
> I don't even have to eat!

John continued by confessing that while everyone was sleeping he crept downstairs and downed a pickled egg, half a dozen cookies, and a green banana. Bennie thought John's problem would be solved when John walked under the Golden Arches and bit into a Big Mac.

"I learned quite a bit from Bennie about the work," John wrote to Gerald, "and have some knowledge of Portuguese. I hope he's gotten some good out of my being here. I've been sick more than half the time and quite lonely for company. I don't want to warm anybody's church bench and I trust the Lord will find something for me to do. I'm planning to return to the States. I could change my mind but this is how it looks to me at the moment."

John's visa extension expired in early June. Although sick often, he had helped the work in Brazil. The preaching pavilion in Compensa barrio that John worked on could seat five hundred people, and another five hundred could stand inside in the wide aisle and altar space. The thatch wall behind the platform and pulpit supported a canopy over this part of the building. Swarms of poor people lived around the area, and Bennie felt they could reach many of them by not getting too sophisticated. If for no other reason, they would come into the building out of curiosity or just because the place looked ugly and they could hear sounds of life inside.

The campaign began. Even on a weeknight with many of the young people in school and no advertising posters put up, no commercial radio announcements, or no broadcasts using announcing on the car's PA system, about four hundred people perched on the benches. There was no way to give directions—the jumble of streets in the new barrio was unnamed or unmarked. By Saturday or Sunday, Bennie expected there would be around one thousand in attendance because each night the people promised to bring friends and relatives.

The financial expense for these things was tremendous. Bennie could only trust the Lord as to how it would all work out, but it seemed that an unlimited future for continuing growth and outlay existed. As encouraging as the spiritual results of these campaigns were, a problem nagged at Bennie. Few people who came to the campaign meetings had a Bible. Bibles were not subsidized and they cost about five dollars each. In just one day, Bennie sold twenty Bibles that he took into the interior pastors.

"We can't let people drift back after a campaign without a follow-up and a way to visit them," Bennie explained. He and Theresa worked out a simple name and address slip to give to those who came to the pavilion. They gathered those up and dropped the names and addresses into a big plastic basket. At the end of each service, they had a small child draw out two names of those who put their name and address in, and they received a Bible. That way the DeMerchants got names and addresses for follow-up calls, and it cost only ten dollars a night.

Even though the weight of deficits hung like an axe suspended over his head, Bennie bought a lot in Manacapuru. Many families living there arrived from surrounding areas to put their kids in school. Bennie felt that without an adequate church the growth would stop, so when a for-sale sign appeared on the property, he grabbed it. The new lot was on the corner of two asphalt streets in the population center of town, in a good area with a future. He had built a wooden church in Manacapuru during his first term, but it was about to fall over. He traded the old one for the new lot, which had both water and electricity. The brethren there would put up a big straw church and use it temporarily until they could build a permanent structure of cement blocks.

The DeMerchants expected the ten students who had gone to Bible school in Rio would be coming home before Christmas. With the growth of the work and the things to do, Bennie wondered where to place them. It seemed he had a tiger by the tail.

Too Many Monkeys, Not Enough Bananas

The "tiger" was snarling. With the present deficits, the work growing so fast, Belém now being Bennie's responsibility, second-generation Pentecostals anxious to go to Bible school, and the possibility of gasoline reaching $4-$5 per gallon in the next year or two—Bennie foresaw a budget of around $8,000-$10,000 per month. He knew it sounded ridiculous, but the only way he'd been able to keep going was to keep the 172 available for hire. In thirty-one months of operation, the 172 earned just over $101,000. Bennie had forty-plus workers or ministers at various levels of responsibility. With about fifteen jobs waiting to be done and with inflation that year going over 55 percent, the DeMerchants were scraping the bottom of the barrel so hard they were putting holes in it.

When one had fifteen or twenty Bible school students returning to their home areas in Amazonas or Pará State needing some form of help to get started, there were just too many monkeys and not enough bananas to go around.

"We don't pay anyone a salary," Bennie told Gerald, "but we do like to see the workers find a job, and we try to help them get something for a building to get started."

The vast northeastern part of Brazil was practically crying for missionary help. Over thirty million Brazilians lived there with an average annual income of $288. Some brethren scattered in that area would function most effectively with a missionary to oversee them, and a great work could be done in a relatively short time. Due to the great distance and outlay of needed money, Bennie felt he couldn't do much more than keep contact with them.

However, in 1980 when Brother Upton returned to Brazil for an evangelistic campaign, Bennie flew with him to Belém where they planned to preach in two small churches. The pastor there maintained himself by selling scrap metal and batteries.

Bennie and Brother Upton stayed in a hotel. At a newsstand in front of the building, Bennie noticed that another missionary group had its official periodical displayed with other newspapers. Bennie bought the pamphlet, but he was so stirred that he had to turn his head away from the man selling the newspapers. Bennie didn't want the vendor to see him crying while he made change.

Why in the world do we boast about what we have done when we have done nothing? Bennie wondered. *One huge denomination in Belém has sixty-eight churches, with many beautiful buildings. An appointed missionary with a large budget who could take to the airwaves is desperately needed here. We might not raise up much that meets the eye, but there would be more people here who would worship the Lord in the Holy Ghost and in truth.*

"Two hundred thirty-two people received the Holy Ghost in this six-week campaign with Brother Upton,"

Theresa wrote Gerald. "The devil is mad about it. Thieves broke into the gallery of our central church upstairs and stole my organ. They pulled the organ and sound box up over the gallery rail with a hose."

In spite of the financially difficult situation, the DeMerchants felt to open up new works on two major Amazon tributaries, the Purús and the Madeira. Some small diesel-powered boats would be a real blessing in those places! The ten bicycles Sheaves for Christ had furnished would put wheels on the work for some rural pastors.

The DeMerchants hoped to pick up many more Partners in Missions as they traveled across the United States and Canada on their approaching furlough. They found a replacement family to live in their house in Manaus while they were on deputation. José Domingues not only had a ministry in evangelization, but was also fluent in Portuguese. Brother Domingues's basic work in Manaus would be to keep things going and to visit as many churches as he could.

Shortly before the DeMerchants left on furlough, Bennie flew to Eirunepé to check on the churches on the western flank. He usually took a load of freshly crated green tomatoes because fresh fruit or vegetables rarely reached the remote town from the outside. The tomatoes would sell quite rapidly and the money from them would just about pay for the gas for the long flight.

A problem arose. The right float on the 172 had opened up while stopped there. Although it had been resealed, it still leaked around the keel; the repairman had neglected to insert two vital screws! Night came on before he reached Carauari, so Bennie landed close to a nearby rubber plantation. The heavy load of tomatoes on the right side forced that leaky float quite low, and it sat with the water nearly level with the top of the back floats.

At 1:00 AM Bennie swung out of his hammock and went outside in the moonlight to check on the plane. He had tied it by the left float to a huge balsa-wood log running out from the muddy riverbank. To Bennie's dismay, the left wing was in the air at a 50-degree angle or more to the horizon. The right float was totally submerged with the right wing resting on the muddy bottom. Bennie slid into the river. Up to his neck in water with about two inches of airspace between water level and fuselage, Bennie could hear the underwater float gurgling away. He scrambled out of the water and into the plane and unloaded the cases of tomatoes in a hurry! Once he slipped off the float and plunged to his neck in the mud, and the case he was carrying escaped his clutch.

Half a dozen houses ringed the small cove where the 172 was tied, so Bennie asked the men in those homes for help. The men rolled from their hammocks and quickly befriended him by dipping into the river for a midnight swim. They untied the ropes from the balsa-wood log and let the current swing the plane around with the front toward the muddy shore.

With a couple of the men holding the right wing off the bottom, a dripping wet Bennie hit full throttle and the wing shot up high and dry while water poured out of it. Leaving the plane there until morning, Bennie crawled back into his hammock and fell asleep. When he returned to the plane in the morning, the errant case of tomatoes was circling around and around in the eddy. They nabbed it as it swirled past the end of the log.

Unfortunately, Bennie had lost his glasses. After diving for an hour looking for them, he persuaded a man who lived close by on the riverbank to hunt for them. The man found the glasses under the balsa log in two meters of water and a meter of mucky bottom mud. A grateful Bennie paid the man with a box of tomatoes. They then reloaded the remaining tomatoes and took to the air again. After reaching Eirunepé, Bennie beached the plane and inserted screws in the two holes.

"Believe me," he wrote Gerald, "the floats are the best ever now. This term has been the best term in every way, and the worst term in every way depending on how one looks at it. But it's time to hit the road again so we'll let the problems sleep with the fathers."

When they returned to Manaus in July 1981 after their fourth furlough, Bennie and Theresa were amazed at how the works had grown while they were away. So much was going on with so many workers and preachers involved that Bennie hardly knew where to start. Between 600 and 650 people came to the central church for their welcome home and for Brother Domingues's farewell service.

The Domingues family with their three teenagers had visited all the places they could reach by road and ministered everywhere they went. They had left the church spiritually sound and growing, so the DeMerchants turned their attention to some other matters. Theresa cleaned the mission house from top to bottom. Termites had freely and generously gorged on one complete closet lining, which had to be removed and replaced. Bennie painted the interior and exterior of the house, and laid a new garage roof—the old one had partially fallen in.

Changes also took place in the daily routines at the home base. Beth and Pam were studying at home on the ACE (Accelerated Christian Education) correspondence course. Bennie liked this because he got to see the girls during the daytime. Beth was very active in the young people's group at the central church and doing very well playing the piano. Pamela rushed through her homework, read a lot of books, and delighted in visiting and riding some horses that one family owned on the other side of Manaus.

Very soon after returning to Manaus, the DeMerchants asked Jack Leaman to dedicate two new church buildings and preach the annual Amazonian convention. At that convention Brother Leaman presented the Faith Promise plan. Five of the city church congregations responded with over $600 a month toward the cost of evangelism outreach. At the same time, pledges were made toward purchasing motors for the boats that the national Brazilian church built and provided.

Then an astounding, truly God thing happened. Bennie had learned early that God could take care of him wherever he was. As a small boy in Canada while sliding on a snow sled, he slid under a freight train that had just started moving. The sled stopped instantly when its steel runners struck the rail. He scrambled out the other side, managing to yank the sled out just before the big boxcar's wheels could crush him.

When he was twelve years old, working on a potato farm, he got his thick overcoat and hands wrapped up in the power takeoff drive shaft of an idling farm tractor's engine connected to a potato digger. Thankfully, his hands were inside the coat and the tractor engine stalled, but his hands hurt for days.

"If the tractor's engine hadn't stalled," his uncle Clem Goodine told him as he kicked the clutch and unwound the stretched skin of fingers and hands, "you could have lost both of your hands or even your life."

Four years later, a teenage Bennie was working with a cement mixer underneath a potato house helping his dad put up new cellar walls. He nearly lost his life when the supports holding the jacked-up house collapsed. He'd crawled out from under the house for a quick breather seconds before the structure crashed down. The next day he helped dig out the flattened cement mixer under the debris of the broken building.

As a missionary, he had fought for his life, buried in an upside-down plane in the Negro River. Never had he faced a more terrifying danger, however, than one he faced in his own garage in Manaus!

Bennie had three barrels of aviation gas on the back of the pickup truck. He backed the truck inside the garage behind the house, and began to siphon the gas into five-gallon plastic containers that Coca-Cola and Pepsi Cola syrup came in. Bennie had siphoned about two barrels of the fuel into the plastic containers when the power went off and plunged the street into darkness. Rather than stop his task, Bennie got a flashlight while Theresa lit candles in the house.

As he siphoned the rest of the gas, he noticed that the liquid from one container had run and spread out in a two-meter diameter on the concrete floor. It was still dark on the street but Bennie kept working anyway. Then he noticed a light behind him. It was his son, Bennie Jonas, who never wanted to be very far away from his dad. Bennie didn't pay much attention because he thought Joe had either another flashlight from the kitchen or the little one that he sometimes took to bed.

However, when Bennie turned around and looked at his son, the little fellow was standing in that puddle of volatile aviation fuel with a lighted candle in his hand!

Bennie shouted, "Get out of here!" and the child lowered his head as he raced down the driveway toward the house. Bennie had once seen aviation gasoline catch fire from a charcoal barbecue over forty-eight feet away and burn one man to death.

Only the hand of the Lord protected us, Bennie thought. *Jonas was right beside me when I looked up and saw that candle.* A trembling Bennie just had to slip away somewhere and thank the Lord for His overshadowing care.

The DeMerchants' intense workload continued. They planned two weeks of seminars for the Amazon preachers. Beth and Theresa worked hard on copying and translating the material from fourteen cassette tapes to printed material in Portuguese. On top of opening two new works, Bennie's several ongoing construction projects included building a new hangar for the airplane. A new boat and motor had to be based in Borba on the Madeira River for working around both sides of a 100-mile-long island. With John Bono gone, Bennie needed a man for A/C maintenance and hangar organization.

As soon as possible, Bennie visited almost all of the thirty churches in the area. Some of these churches had joint services where people could come by boat from nearby, usually within twenty to thirty miles. In the suburban area of Manaus, Pastor Raimundo was expanding his church from an outgrown building that would seat two hundred people to one that would seat up to six hundred. The church folk contributed not only their own work on the building, but also funded it. They never asked for a dime for construction materials.

Other obvious improvements thrilled the DeMerchants' hearts. In Parintins a concrete foundation had been laid for a new block building. In Pauini, 650 miles up the Purús River southwest of Manaus, the saints were getting ready to construct a new church. Bennie remembered when he left Brother Janio in Pauini. A serious, single young man, Janio jumped hurriedly into the back of the seaplane at Bennie's suggestion on a fuel stop going upriver at Caapiranga. Pauini, a small town totally isolated far up on the Purús River, had had no pastor for some time. Bennie left Janio over the weekend to encourage the church. As he stepped out on the pontoon of the plane, the young man looked a bit disoriented at the suddenness of being left alone in a strange town. When the fellow said he did not have a hammock, Bennie tossed him his own. (A hammock is a portable rope bed wherever one sleeps even if in a five-star hotel using their hammock hooks set in the concrete walls, or out in the boonies stringing it between two trees.) When Bennie returned four days later to pick Janio up, he found that the local people loved Janio and were begging him to stay. He was from a family of diligent workers and Bennie knew if Janio stayed he would build up a work. The first person to be baptized in that town was the town judge!

When Bennie returned to Pauini a few months later, Janio had married one of the hard-working, serious church girls and was working with her father building boats and running a small store and bakery. Janio continued pastoring the local church, built a large boat of his own for evangelizing the villages up and down the river, and later opened up a food store. As time went on, he opened a Bible school, enlarged the local church three times, built a huge church and has the largest store in town. He helps other workers open up new works and supports them. God has blessed him. Today, his name and the church he pastors are well known over that area of the huge Purús River.

Nowadays, when Bennie and other visitors fly in from a six-hour flight and splash down, Janio sends a boat to pick them up, has a car waiting at the edge of the river, feeds them a big, well-prepared meal, and sees that they get a great night's sleep in his air-conditioned second floor hotel suite beside the local airport. He laughs in front of a fully loaded table prepared by his hard-working wife, reminding them that it all started by hopping into the back of Bennie's Cessna seaplane nearly twenty years earlier when he finished Bible school and wanted to go out on an evangelistic caravan without much extra clothing and not even a hammock.

As before, the mercy flights for the Brazilian government continued. On one of his trips for FUNAI he ran into a group of partially-westernized Indians who had been reached with a Christian group and most of them had received the Holy Ghost. Their women dressed modestly compared with other groups. They were begging for Bibles. Many of them spoke Portuguese, so Bennie planned to buy some Portuguese Bibles and bring them some literature the next time he visited. As with other such groups, he did everything low key, praying for the day when he could openly teach the message on his heart.

Eirunepé is on the upper Juruá River at the junction with the Tarauacá River. It is a fifteen-minute hop over to Jutai and an hour and fifteen minutes to upper Solimões River. All of these had large isolated towns where the work could grow. Sometimes Bennie mixed flying for FUNAI with his own interests. He overnighted on many of these trips where he also had churches and ministered to the saints there while the officials registered in a hotel. He scouted ranches with hundreds of heads of cows or noted rubber plantations with a small village of working people to evangelize later.

By early 1983, the DeMerchants were able to report some happy problems to Harry Scism, director of Foreign Missions. When they had arrived in 1965, Manaus had been just a sprawling, unorganized town of about one hundred eighty thousand people. Then the federal government of Brazil made the town a free zone with exemptions on imports for tourists and industrial projects in the area. By 1983 the city numbered over one million inhabitants.

A huge area of Manaus consisted of about three hundred thousand people. From the air this section of town looked like an anthill. A new street called Avenida Brazil bisected this poor section. The oldest wooden church in Manaus stood close by. Bennie, in planning for future growth, felt that a new, large central tabernacle in this area should seat about thirty-five hundred people. In addition to the auditorium, he wanted a place to sell Bibles and literature. He also foresaw the need for space for correspondence courses to combine with a radio program. Bennie estimated the cost for that type of building would be about $35,000. It could be built in two phases: the first phase would seat about two thousand people, and the second phase would come later on. Unfortunately, the funds he had garnered while on furlough had already been depleted. The same old problem remained: too many monkeys, not enough bananas.

So he added another monkey: a nice evangelism boat for the Madeira River. Twelve meters long, it would hold about twelve tons. With a pastor and workers in a new central area on the Madeira, they could haul forty or fifty people, barrels of aviation gas, sand, cement, blocks, or whatever, for constructing simple churches. A pastor and his family could live on board and make chain visits to various churches in the region, strengthening them. The latest boat was the sixth, and Bennie felt that such boats really paid off.

Now to find more bananas.

When one does not have the funds to buy an aluminum boat: the Indians make them from hardwood straight tree trunks.

Pastor Altemiro Cordoso and his wife—in Eirunepé ministering since 1975

Home of Bennie and Theresa DeMerchant in Manaus

Memories of a Strut

At the end of a sheltered cove near Manaus, a well-anchored floating hangar off the main river provided a place where Bennie could keep and maintain the aircraft out of the wind and waves of passing rain squalls. One day after a heavy rain shower with strong winds had passed, Bennie, with Bennie Joe as his only passenger, taxied the Cessna 172 seaplane at idle to warm up the engine prior to takeoff. As Bennie applied full power for takeoff while still in the sheltered cove area, the seaplane sped up to ski with a long white "rooster tail" of water behind. Still gaining speed, the 172 rapidly approached the rough water at the end of the cove where the wind changed abruptly, necessitating a much longer water run before takeoff.

As Bennie skied away from the shelter of the cove, he spotted whitecaps ahead, a no-no for takeoff. With a glance at the air speed indicator, Bennie realized the plane could not lift above the water soon enough. He instantly cut power, but before the plane stopped, it skidded and bounced through some high waves.

The attachment end of one of the struts, descending from the front of the aircraft to its left float, cracked. When the strut cracked, a straining rod that helped hold the plane upright also broke, and the left wing dropped beyond its normal position.

"Dad, why are you turning back toward the floating hangar?" Bennie Joe asked.

"After going around the turn, I saw that the water in the bay was too rough, so I aborted the takeoff," Bennie explained.

Bennie was thankful for shelter from the hot sun as he replaced the strut with another he had on reserve. As he dismounted the perfectly straight strut, he saw that the fitting on its end was cracked and bent. He thought to himself, *If this strut could talk of the places it has already been, what a story it would tell!*

Later, when asked to write an article for Sheaves for Christ (SFC), Bennie penned some highlights of what that strut had seen in its "lifetime" of service.

Memories of a Strut

I would like to tell you of some of the highlights of my past twelve year lifetime. I am a two-pound, 29-inch hardened aluminum strut or support that has held the left float in position on the SFC Brazilian floatplane for the last ten years in Amazonas, Brazil.

After forty-five hours of flying from St. Paul, Minnesota, I arrived in June of 1971 in Manaus, Brazil. Since that time, I would guess that I have been up and down over twelve thousand times. I have seen the infinite string of luxury hotels below on the eastern coast of Florida; the sky-blue and orange coral reefs of the Bahamas; St. Lucia Island poking up out of the Atlantic Ocean like a mountain; and the solid green Amazon jungle sweeping to the far horizon in all directions. I have flown out of busy air terminals such as Miami, and splashed down on far-out jungle lakes where alligators' snouts eased under the water. I have bored through solid fog that left water droplets clinging on my aft side or sliced through sheets of rain that turned the windshield gray and obliterated the view of the wingtips.

I was there in silence

while the general superintendent and the director of Foreign Missions stepped by me to officiate the groundbreaking services of a new church on Marrecão Island in the Amazon River 45 miles upstream from Manaus;

while Bennie and others climbed the fallen tree's trunk leading up over the bank of the Alalaú River to stand in shock over the remains of massacred government workers killed by a savage Atroaris Indian attack in 1974;

while an ambulance answered a radio call from the airport in Manaus to pick up a critical accident victim from an interior town at a local ferry landing;

while a missionary's six-year-old son, who had fallen off a boat in the Amazon River during a night boat trip and was found drowned and floating the next day, wrapped in a sheet, and loaded in the rear while his older brother and dad wept;

while a victim of a poisonous snakebite was carried in a hammock and put aboard and flown in the night for medical help and life-saving precautions, only to return in a wooden box;

while a doctor and thousands of vaccines on

ice were loaded to control an epidemic in the border area of Waupes River;

while thousands of tracts, cases of new Bibles, and Portuguese songbooks were loaded for a chain of visits into the jungle churches in the interior of the state;

while the first 43 people of the newly opened church in Maués were baptized in Jesus' name beside me, or 31 in Marrecão, 10 on Black Lake, 18 on the Amazon's Paratari Island and many, many other places hard to even remember;

while the Lord baptized 28 with the Holy Ghost in a straw thatch-roofed church on Maçoari Lake, 11 others in Cameta village, 24 more in the crooked and narrow Eirú River in the jungle, and in the St. Antonio Creek church where my pilot wasn't too pilot-ish, jumping for joy on the platform while 17 prayed through to their Pentecostal experience with Brother Upton present;

while the missing pastor with a broken-down motorboat was found after a dozen or more takeoffs and landings to ask folks along the river for information as to where the pastor might be.

Though short, my life has been a good one and I have seen the churches in Brazil's central Amazon River area grow from three to thirty and hundreds receive their water and Spirit baptism. In this Amazonas State the work covers a twelve-hundred-mile stretch of rivers, lakes, jungle, and villages. Some forty-three licensed ministers pastor the region, and more are appearing and maturing.

At high speeds, water even with small waves can be very hard. A few days ago, while planing on the water at about 60 mph, the aircraft rounded a point of land and I was struck with higher waves than I like. Immediately Bennie shut down the horses, but before coming to a stop and returning to my origin in the sheltered cove, one-half of my fuselage connection support cracked. The incident ruined my perfection. As you know, in aviation only the perfect is acceptable, so I must go down to an aluminum graveyard. A new strut will take my place. I have been a supporter all my life; it was my duty.

And you? Will you continue to support SFC?

SFC purchased the 172 Cessna seaplane in September 1970 that after ten thousand hours of operation still flies today in 2015.

The "Wood" in the Woods

Scientists all over the world are protesting the savage destruction of vast areas of the Amazon's tropical rainforest. Trees are cut as roads and subsequent agricultural projects follow in the brush burner's wake. The Amazon Basin, larger than the USA, is called the "Green Hell," the world's largest natural "oxygen factory," the "lungs" of the world. Environmentalists claim this tree-cutting on a large scale is upsetting the world's climate patterns. In far-off places, they say this is felt by severe or mild winters, drought, or floods.

The work of the Lord in Brazil could well be compared to a forest or woods. The UPCI missionaries in Brazil were excited about what the Lord was doing in this "woods" of people. In São Paulo's national UPCB convention, waves of glory swept over the congregation night after night. Over fifty were filled with the Holy Ghost. In a Sunday afternoon baptismal service, the Holy Ghost fell and many, one by one, as they stepped into the baptismal tank, threw up their hands and worshiped the Lord. Facial expressions flashed to joy as they spoke with other tongues and glorified the Lord. Soon those standing in line started to receive it, and even those in the waiting room waiting to be baptized were filled as they too were swept into the kingdom of God.

Dozens of truth-loving students who had graduated from the Apostolic Bible Institute in Rio de Janeiro had left school and taken their Holy Ghost powered buzz saws into the Amazon region of Brazil where they were in active ministry. Many of them were cutting down "big timber" for the name of the Lord Jesus!

In working with the Lord, one never knows what He is going to do. In anticipation of a great move of God, Bennie once again invited Leo Upton to come to Manaus. They visited twenty-six churches in their area, mostly by floatplane, and before he left, 232 people had received their gift from the Lord—the baptism of the Holy Ghost, speaking in other tongues for the first time.

In the city of the Manacapuru, just twenty-five minutes flying time west from Manaus, they built a Holy Ghost kit. It was nothing more than a palm-thatch-roofed pavilion that was built to seat 450 people. But Satan's ecologists were not about to accept this "timber felling" without putting up a good struggle.

Bennie had never seen so many things go wrong on one construction site in all his life as he did when they tried to get the pavilion up and ready in time for the special services. They started out by getting a front-end loader to level the lot. In the slippery clay it got stuck in the mud. The battery ran down. The fuel system got plugged. Then it ran out of fuel. The gas station had no diesel fuel. Although they got some fuel that night, the next day the business was closed. The truck broke down on the jungle road. They sent another truck to pull it in, and the hitch snapped when it was towed. It ended up off the road in the swamp. It seemed as if hornets were stinging them all the time and while they resolved one problem three more took its place. Even the alternator and the radio went out on the floatplane. But like a thermometer, one can sense future victory by the degree to which their efforts are frustrated, and several times Bennie told Brother Upton that something good was coming.

After the last board was nailed on top of the stakes that were driven into the mud floor of this pavilion and the lightbulbs were strung overhead, they were ready to go with services. In the opening services that weekend in Manacapuru, fifty-three received the baptism of the Holy Ghost and thirty were baptized in water in Jesus' name.

Seven hundred sixty-five miles west, on the Eirú River in the local town of Eirunepé the following weekend, thirty-one more were added to the kingdom of God by the same experience. One hundred sixty-five miles north of Manaus on the Trans-Amazon Highway, one man received the Holy Ghost while walking down the aisle to the altar. Then 165 miles east of Manaus at Maués, twenty-two received the Holy Ghost. One hundred twenty miles south of Manaus at Saint Rita, where Bennie slid the floatplane down into a narrow river channel, sixteen received the Holy Ghost.

That night the natives clubbed a poisonous snake to death almost under Brother Upton's hammock. In the commotion of killing the snake, the natives worked by a flashlight's beam and never even woke him up, so as not to ruin his sleep. Bennie didn't awaken until the next morning. Literally everywhere—north, south, east, or west—God was pouring out His spirit on Amazonians. They received it in the audience, walking to the altar, standing up, or sitting down. On Brother Upton's third trip to the Amazon over six hundred people received the baptism of the Holy Ghost.

After seeing twenty-two pray through one night, Bennie gritted his teeth in a frown when he looked down and saw a $700 amplifier spewing out smoke. He quickly pulled the plug. The transformer in it had burned out. From his position on the floor of the platform, he looked out over that audience and saw all those new people drunken in their newly found Holy Ghost experience. None of them could care less about this world just then and so Bennie said to himself, "I don't care either. I will praise the Lord anyhow and fix it tomorrow."

In thinking about the thousands of people who lived in the Amazon, Bennie realized he would never run out of "wood." He promised himself to keep his power saw sharpened with plenty of gas in its tank.

Go Ahead, Laugh!

After the long hassle with Brazil's restricting laws and protocols, the Cessna 206 floatplane was finally released for importation to Brazil. This new Cessna replaced the one lost in the accident that took the lives of Margaret Calhoun and José Cinque. Now, five years later, they had a second plane legally imported and registered in Brazil.

However, if they lost their aircraft or if it had to be grounded for a time from lacking a part or because of inspection overhaul, they would need a backup. Since the resale value on their small Cessna 172 floatplane (which had gone through four engines and had over fifty thousand miles on it) was negligible, the Foreign Missions Board wisely allowed them to keep the 172 for backup service. The DeMerchants depended on their "flying boat" for working their twenty-one-hundred-mile-wide district of rivers and rainforest.

Bennie had installed a new man with his family in Carauari. In two months the worker had reached over fifty people, and half of those had been baptized in Jesus' name. Large amounts of natural gas and petroleum were discovered near this city five hundred miles west of Manaus on the Juruá River and the area was booming. Bennie decided to take their national executive secretary with him on a nine-day, circuit-rider-type trip to check out the new work and visit the brethren and other churches in that area, preaching almost every night. One time during a two-day stretch, they landed twenty-six times! The secretary had to leave early, so Bennie sent him back to Manaus on a commercial flight while he continued the spiritual checkup.

On his own return after two and a half hours flying over solid jungle, Bennie spotted an isolated lake with good black water that indicated the possibility of tucunaré, known as peacock bass. He dropped the plane into this remote lake just to do something different. Pulling his fly rod from its holder, he climbed on top of the fuselage behind the windshield to throw the line over the plane's antennas to flip the lure into the water. After a few casts, he changed his mind. There were too many gator snouts around. Bennie counted six gators that charged off a mudbank when they saw him and made underwater bubbles in this dry season's small, shallow isolated lake. Their action put them a bit too close for him to enjoy fly-rodding. He knew some of those bigger gators could get mean!

The DeMerchants' children were growing up too fast to suit Bennie and Theresa. Beth would be graduating from the St. Paul ABI on the next furlough, and Pam would be going there the following fall. BJ was quite active, full of questions, very God conscious, and believed everything Bennie told him. The boy was crazy about Jeeps and liked them even better than airplanes.

Every fall, the pastors, workers, and congregations in general met for a conference. The central church in Manaus, which would hold around eight hundred people, was in the process of a building program. Bennie was racing against time to get the building finished. The nine local churches in Manaus had to consolidate their choirs rather than let each have time of its own. Beth assembled a nice sixty-voice master choir and had them ready for the conference. She helped her parents gather into two booklets all the Search for Truth lessons with their illustrations and drawings for ten lessons in Portuguese. In addition, they put together their first United Pentecostal Church of Brazil (UPCB) manual, which included national district and local church constitutions. Everyone then could know in writing what was expected of them.

Shortly after the conference, a virus of some kind swept through northern Brazil, causing eyes to swell and turn red. The virus was very painful, especially for the first three days, and spread quite rapidly. It got to Bennie. It felt as if someone had thrown sand in his eyes, and if he rubbed them, they hurt worse. He hunted all the drugstores for some medicine for relief. He finally found what he wanted and bought twenty doses just to give to the people in the interior. After going to Eirunepé and distributing it, he ran out of the medicine after the second stop. Bennie felt the Lord allowed him to catch the virus so he could empathize with the afflicted and get some medicine for the pastors and workers. Only wearing the darkest sunglasses and putting drops in his eyes every thirty minutes brought relief. Fortunately, even though the problem lasted for ten days, by the end of the third day with red eyes, the worst was over.

For a long time the DeMerchants had desired a new typewriter. When Bennie saw IBM typewriters at a special promotional price, he bought one for Theresa's birthday. They liked the eraser type ribbon, which made the errors come off fast. They now had a more modern device with which to start up a national paper in Portuguese, something they felt was badly needed for communication between the workers and pastors.

The plane fund had fallen through the bottom. So when FUNAI wanted him to do a complete run of Amazonas State in the Cessna 206, he was happy to do so. He would be overjoyed to replenish the nonexistent fund and have money left over for building funds. He had requests from all over asking for help to build but he just didn't have the cash. By the Lord's help he wanted to push some of their good men into more unreached areas. He also desired to help those with boats who were going to towns in some of those new places. Those hard workers only asked for the boat, motor, and a little fuel. They kept working away while all Bennie could do was ask them to wait a little longer for the supplies they needed. Then they got welcome help from an unexpected source: Clayton Goodine.

Bennie's cousin, affectionately called "Uncle" Clayton, visited Manaus to teach a seminar on leadership. He and Bennie flew out to some of the interior churches before and after the meetings. The floating church on balsa logs intrigued Clayton. The congregation of over one hundred inside really knew how to worship! He admired the women with small children leaving church after dark to paddle a couple of miles with their babies. When Clayton returned to his home in New Brunswick, he raised funds for a boat and motor project and sent the money to Bennie's account.

The riverside cities and towns usually spread out on the highest land available along the riverbanks. When the dry season hits, the river level can fall as much as 60-65 feet. During the rainy season, many of the low islands and other areas on the huge Amazon flood easily. The Amazon then is called by mariners the "Inland Sea." At very high water levels, even Manaus, the capital, can have streets near the river with water deep enough to paddle a canoe down them. The stores in this area sandbag the entrances and place their stock on shelves or elevated pallets to be above the water level.

Cattle and buffalo ranchers transfer their livestock on huge wooden barges to higher ground sometimes fifty miles away. They rent the highland pastures for their animals to survive for months while the water recedes and the ground dries out enough to produce new grassland. Many of the people who live in houses in these areas build their wooden houses on stilts two meters above the land and during this time prefer to live with relatives on higher ground. Anacondas may be swept down the flooded river at night to lodge around the stilts of these houses, so women living alone with babies often choose to move in with other family members elsewhere.

There are several villages of just floating houses built on balsa wood or lighter weight, resin-filled high floating logs. Floating churches are built to solve the problem of reaching people in these areas that flood for long periods of the year. All Amazonians know how to swim and paddle a canoe at a very early age since canoes are their main means of transportation. At the floating church, canoes paddle up in the dark with a flashlight and moon to guide them. They nose up along the walkway around the church so their family members can step up from the canoe on the walkway. Often mothers bring their small children without clothes on and dress the kids on the walkway before entering the building. The church may have a small gasoline or diesel powered lighting plant to operate the electric guitars and sound system, which usually is a soundbox.

As the church loads up with people, its logs sink deeper and deeper into the water. Bennie has been in services that when the altar call was given and people surged to the front, the change of weight caused the altar area to go underwater sometimes up to two or three palm spans. The people are barefooted or wear flip-flop sandals and are used to standing in the water. When the congregation outgrows the church, the building can be sold to buy a larger one or towed to another location if it sits on a lake with no current. If a floating church is untied from its mooring on the river, it is all but impossible to pull it upstream due to the strong current.

Not long after the seminar with Clayton Goodine, a group of six ministers and their wives spent three days in Manaus. One of the ministers had brought some items from the States. As a thank you, Bennie dropped into the hotel's beachfront and picked them up to take them for a ride over the city. Later they went with Theresa and BJ on a riverboat trip from the hotel to the meeting of the waters where the Rio Negro joins the Amazon. The boat ride took them into the jungle to see huge lily pads, anaconda snake handlers, and some live gators. Bennie teased them by saying it might be easier on them at judgment day if they all had taken on the DeMerchants as Partners in Missions.

One of the Brazilian ministers developed a unique way of reaching people. In Coari, Manoel Magalhaes and his wife were having success teaching Search for Truth in home Bible studies. Other religious groups in the town forbade their members to visit Brother Manoel's church and vigorously opposed them. After losing some of his members, one such pastor insisted that members of his church not even open their doors to a Oneness person.

So Brother Manoel took to the streets. He had a baptismal tank in the church but wouldn't use it. Instead, he took a big blackboard right out in front of a street market early in the morning when the market was closed to vehicle traffic and animatedly taught an illustrated Bible lesson. Curious folk gathered around to watch—and listen—and become convinced they needed the Lord. Brother Manoel would slip down over the riverbank and baptize the new converts, sometimes someone from another church. He often stood in the water and preached

110

to a good-sized crowd. He loved to take the blackboard for street meetings as well. The other pastors couldn't stop people from walking on the streets or going to the market! And every week someone prayed through to the Holy Ghost. Even with such opposition, the Coari church had over one hundred fine people, most of whom were Spirit-filled and water-baptized. The denominational groups had laughed when Brother Manoel built a large, cement block church with so many pews, but his church was filling rapidly and he had not been there much over a year.

The priest of the Roman Catholic Church owned the local radio station and used the airwaves to lambast the Pentecostal fanatics. People who lived on boats in the interior paddled for days to look up the church out of curiosity because they had heard so much they couldn't believe. One denominational pastor grew furious when he visited one of his members and found Manoel there. He told Manoel to shut up and get out. Manoel never moved.

"I'm a Brazilian and live under a constitution," Manoel calmly replied. "I was invited to this home by a new member of my church who has been baptized."

The pastor had no answer for that!

When Bennie, Theresa, BJ, and some of the ministers from Manaus went to dedicate the new church in Coari, nearly two hundred people crowded into the structure. Other denominations, the Spiritualists, and the local priest were up in arms because every week Pastor Manoel baptized new people and these soon received the Holy Ghost. The Sunday night dedication service lasted four hours, and eleven were baptized in water and nine received the Holy Ghost.

People may have laughed at Manoel Magalhaes for building such a large cement block structure. They snickered at the big number of pews—pews they were sure would stay empty. But with Search for Truth, street meetings, good teaching, and printed matter liberally distributed, all those pews filled up fast.

The hecklers stopped laughing.

Theresa and BJ in rural Amazon church service

Seaplane and dugout canoes

Going to church the Amazonian way!

Go East, Young Man

Shortly after the dedication of the church in Coari, Bennie and some workers flew in the opposite direction to Pará State and Belém, its capital, to check out about a dozen Oneness congregations that were looking to them for guidance and help. Bennie felt it was beyond his means to oversee and direct such an operation. The area was too big to add to the vast Amazonas State and nearly the same size. More than that, Belém was as far east as Eirunepé was west.

One day he met a pastor in the church in Parintins at the border between Amazonas and Pará State. The pastor told Bennie he had immigrated from Egypt to Brazil along with his parents when he was twelve years old and he was healed of total blindness. Later he started preaching with an Adventist group and even went to their seminary for four years. Then he received the Holy Ghost.

"One day I was using a concordance and discovered that baptism in water in the Bible was only administered in Jesus' name," he said. "I pointed out what I had found to two other preachers. They saw the truth and accepted it. Then they baptized each other in Jesus' name. Now, many small, isolated groups in Pará State baptize in Jesus' name."

Unfurling a map, he showed Bennie more than a dozen places he had been where people baptized in Jesus' name. After hearing this, Bennie decided to take some ministers and a load of tracts and other materials and fly the two thousand miles between Manaus and Belém in dogleg stops and visit some of those towns on the lower Amazon River.

Almost half of Bennie's flying outside of church work was to help in rescue cases or to supply medical aid. He got a call one night to fly to Ponta Alegre village on the Andirá River near Parintins. A woman there had been unconscious for seven hours due to childbirth complications. The baby had swung crosswise and was pushing up hard on the woman's lungs, causing very difficult breathing. The woman was paralyzed and labor had stopped for several hours. Bennie realized the woman would not be able to sit up so he slid the two seats on the right of the pilot off their rails. A few hundred onlookers had gathered in the light of a half moon to watch as four men holding the ends of the hammock she was lying in lifted her into this space. The woman's husband sat on the floor with her head in his lap and held the woman's arms to keep them from hitting him in the neck.

At that late hour it would be difficult to get any attention in a maternity ward in Manaus, a two-and-a-half-hour flight away. Instead, Bennie banked the plane toward Parintins, a town of about seventy thousand people with a hospital. After securing the plane at the bank of the river in Parintins in the dark, Bennie reached a suburb of the town and searched for a taxi while the husband stayed in the plane, holding the gasping, struggling, sweat-doused woman. Bennie finally found a taxi, and with the other man's help, got her to the hospital. The staff there immediately called the doctor, who roared up on a motorcycle and operated soon after arriving. After spending the night at a hotel,

Bennie called the hospital the next morning and learned that the woman was conscious and cuddling a baby girl.

The ups and downs, particularly downs, of the Brazilian economy greatly affected the poor people. The fifteen-year-old daughter of one of their preachers died quite suddenly of rheumatic fever. The family didn't even have money for a burial box so Bennie paid for one since the family had been loyal for many years. A nice funeral was held in the central church. Bennie spoke about attitudes and used Job as an example of how, in spite of all his loss, Job worshiped God instead of cursing Him.

The following week Bennie flew to Nhamundá. Supplies that had arrived earlier from Manaus needed to be skipped over the watershed to the central Wai-Wai Indian village on the Mapueira River. Intervening rapids on the river caused the place to be very difficult to be reached by land or river. The land across from Nhamundá rose sharply to form the watershed. On the other side, rocks dammed the Mapueira and shaped a pond on which he could safely drop the plane. He hopped five tons of supplies, food stuffs, and salt in thirty-minute runs from Nhamundá to the Wai-Wai tribe populating the Mapueira's banks.

After he splashed down, he met a very fine older lady, Irene Benson. This dedicated single woman from Indiana, USA, had lived with this tribe forty years, spoke their language fluently, and had taught Portuguese to their children in school since the tribe's arrival from Guiana.

Bennie cried as he heard her story of a huge forest fire that had burned through the area in the dry summer season ruining their crops of manioc, corn, and vegetables, leaving the Indians without an immediate source of food. The dry season had lowered the water level. There was little refrigeration and no diesel fuel to run the light plant. With over a thousand Indians there drawing fish from the river, population pressure had reduced fishing in the river to nearly nothing.

However, the tribe could send boats upriver beyond their normal fishing range. From these upriver places they could catch fish, fillet and salt it in the dry-season sun, and preserve it till making the long trip back. The vital salt, dried grains, and jerricans of diesel fuel were urgently needed to bolster the food supply. Bennie knew he would be out a few barrels of aviation fuel but this situation was one of those many times when the flying boat had to kick in and help needy people, knowing that one day it would all come back.

On one of those runs over the jungle section, the 206 started to strain. Nothing Bennie did to regulate the fuel mixture helped. As soon as he could, he found a safe place to land. Scrounging tools from his ever-present aviation toolbox, he took the fuel strainers apart and discovered they were fairly clogged up with lint, fine hair, sand, and chamois fuzz. After he cleaned them out, he resumed the flight.

Later in the same week, a dry windstorm hit the hangar where Bennie kept his planes and swept almost half the roof into the middle of the lake. The roof truss dropped on top of the little plane and broke out a Plexiglas window in the baggage compartment. A 2' x 4' went through the windshield. Fellows from the shop installed a locally bought piece of Plexiglas that they heated and bent for the back window. A brace in the middle of the back window had been broken by the truss, but they substituted one of equal size from a different plane and riveted it in. Bennie installed a new windshield and observed, "Around here when you don't have a dog you hunt with your cat."

Then the Indian Department called on Bennie to take a load of supplies to some of the wildest and most culturally isolated Indians in the Amazon. Bennie set up an intercept with some anthropologists on the Tapauá River and sent fuel on ahead by boat. A four-hour run southwest in the 206 would take them to the Tapauá River, a tributary of the Purús River. Even though some of the anthropologists had nearly lost their lives during a previous encounter with this group on the Riozinho that flows into the Tapauá, they were to present a final report to the government on the numbers in the tribe and its location in order to mark out a reserve area to protect them. Only 120 Indians were recorded as living in the area, but Bennie flew over the area for three hours and found seven large, round community houses in the middle of the jungle. When Bennie and the five agents with him found an active house, they saw naked Indians rush into the clearing, waving axes over their heads. Some of the Indians had bows that were longer than they were tall.

The people with him in the 206 were filming and making notes and taking compass headings for ways to get there on the ground. They warned Bennie not to go lower, so he maintained an altitude around 800 feet and saw two Indians shoot arrows toward the plane. He watched the arrow streak 200 to 300 feet toward the plane, slow down, stall, and fall back toward the ground below. Checking his ever-present Day Timer's pocket agenda, he noted that at that same time the UPCI 1984 General Conference was being held in Anaheim, California!

A few days later two women who worked with Wycliffe Bible Translators called on Bennie to fly to a tribe on the Uneixi River where they were working about 450 miles northwest of Manaus. They had a very sick Indian woman who had had a high fever for two days. Normally, Bennie didn't fly for the Wycliffe translators, but the plane they usually used had crashed a few months earlier on a jungle strip and they needed something that would land on water. They were stranded for transportation, and seeing how his

PIM account needed an infusion of cash, Bennie answered their call.

Bennie debated with himself and discussed with the ladies whether he should take the sick Indian woman out or leave her there. The translators had no medical experience and couldn't even find a vein for administering intravenous fluids. They found some oral medication and mixed it up. Bennie had them bring her in her hammock and put her in the copilot seat since it was the only seat that reclined. Her husband climbed into the plane and sat behind her. It was more than ninety-five degrees on the surface so Bennie climbed to an altitude where the air temperature was sixty degrees to help cool her body. Occasionally Bennie spooned some of the oral medication into her mouth. Even though she was unconscious, she would swallow it. Bennie hoped the solution would help through the four-and-one-half-hour flying time to Manaus, but as he flew the plane through a rain front, the woman stopped breathing. While her husband looked on from the backseat, Bennie pumped her chest a few times and she came back again for just a minute. Sadly, she died in flight.

When Bennie reached the VHF range, he decided to report the incident in case the authorities opened up an inquiry. When he did so he advised them that an Indian lady aboard had passed away. He gave them the telephone number for the Indian Department for arrangements with an ambulance at the ferry crossing on the Rio Negro on the west side of Manaus. The VHF radio and control tower operator called FUNAI and passed on the information Bennie had given him. When the 206 taxied into shore, a crowd had gathered to watch the dead woman be pulled out of the plane and onto a stretcher.

"That was the first time I hopelessly watched someone die," Bennie wrote to Gerald. That day he saw more clearly where his efforts directly and indirectly saved hundreds of lives. The precious medical supplies the government requested that he deliver often relieved an epidemic of some kind in Indian tribes near the Venezuelan, Colombian, or Peruvian border on narrow headwaters of tributaries flowing through the jungle.

Bennie tried never to make more than fuel and wear and tear expenses on other flying missions because they were missions too, and maybe one day he might need them to rescue him from the jungle. Helping and making friends with anyone is a good policy. On the other hand, government missions usually involved a lot of time and long distances on these nearly impossible runs. Anything could happen out in the sparsely populated jungle areas. If Bennie were to make these long runs to the heads of rivers in border areas, he had to charge a good price because of risk. If a problem with the plane developed, it could take weeks to return to it with replacement parts and maybe a mechanic or two. It could mean an interminable boat ride or chartering an airplane from other friends.

The Indians on the Abonari River were now westernized enough to run video cameras and drive vehicles. Pressure was placed on the government to mark Indian reserves to avoid conflicts over land, jurisdiction, and privileges. Surveyors slashed a six-meter-wide swath through the jungle and placed markers along Indian reserve border areas.

Using power saws, axes, and machetes, one surveyor team was working in the most remote bush area of their huge reserve. Some of the men had a serious accident and needed medication. Infection had set in and the injured workers were in an impossible-to-reach place almost on the equator in the sweltering heat of the jungle. No way could they be carried out. After they made radio contact with their base in Manaus, an army helicopter was sent to find them, but it had to turn back when its fuel ran low.

It was a long run for the little 172, but on June 26, 1985, after refueling at the FUNAI outpost near the present bridge over the Alalaú River, Bennie followed the ever-narrowing river to its headwaters where it broke up into small unnavigable streams under the green jungle canopy. The survey team marking the boundary of this Indian reserve was camped at the head of this river.

Most people in the woods who are lost know they need a smoky fire signal to billow up through the trees, Bennie thought. *These surveyors would surely know I'm looking for their smoke.* He had little reserve fuel to go farther and in fifteen more minutes of flying would reach his point of no return.

Could these men in the jungle hear the soft, smooth putt-putt-putt of a Cessna 172 in cruise? Maybe not. So before turning back, Bennie put the plane in a full throttle climb and slowly circled the rippling green sea of jungle below. He hoped the exhaust pipe, turned outward in the turn and revved up high would wake up at least a few monkeys and jaguars. His eyes raked the horizon. Nothing.

Give them more time to get the fire going, he thought. Bennie was well into the second 360-degree climbing turn when far to the east he spotted a little puffball of smoke. Minutes later he passed over their heads and like a bomber pilot on his run, dropped a plastic sack with medical supplies into the center of their small clearing near their waving hands.

Later in the day, a couple of officers from the military base knocked at the door of the DeMerchant home to confirm a rumor they had heard.

"Did you or did you not reach those folks in the jungle and make an air drop?" they wanted to know.

Bennie acknowledged that the rumor was true. Strapping his body to a flying seat with wings was not only work and fun, but at times it brought great satisfaction.

Meanwhile, work on the rivers below the wings of the floatplane continued at a rapid pace. The UPCB sent a new evangelism boat with a firsthand diesel engine for a Madeira River pastor who had graduated from the ABI in Rio and had migrated to Borba. He had a hard time for a while. As he was preaching on the street, a thrown rock almost the size of a fist hit him on the head and knocked him down.

The church lot sat on a pocket of low land. When rainy season struck, water converted it to a pond and church benches floated around until the city built a drain for the area. A rival denomination had a nice church in town that seated between eight hundred and one thousand members. They did their best to run him out. They even had special prayer meetings for the Lord to close his work, but the rival church's work went down to half a dozen on Sunday night, and the brother's church filled up.

Now, with this boat added to his evangelization arsenal, the pastor could visit a church three hours upriver where sometimes he had waited four days to return to Borba on the line boat. Folks in other new areas were beckoning to him, asking him to bring some of his church people to visit, preach, and fellowship.

When Bennie opened a three-month training session for two nights a week, eighty men registered for the classes. Three-quarters of them bused in after work to attend on Mondays and Fridays, off nights for churches in Manaus. On this convenient schedule, students came from all the churches in Manaus. Such a schedule was convenient for Bennie too. He didn't need to house or feed the students because they could be gone thirty minutes after class and do homework in their own homes.

Bennie used the "Gospels, Acts, and Epistles" tract that S. G. Norris had written for use at ABI in St. Paul, Minnesota. On Monday night he taught for two hours from the tract. Then on Friday night he reviewed the material for an hour before giving the students a hard, tricky test. Bennie figured the best student would score an 80 or so on it. The students had a lot of references and things to memorize, but one man scored a 99 and several others had scores in the 90s.

"They must have photographic memories," Bennie informed Gerald, "because I made them put their Bibles and all their notes on the platform. There is no telling the potential there and it does me good to see all of them listening closely and writing down everything they can."

Solving the problem of training men locally, however, caused another problem: they were going to have to build another church—the tenth—in Manaus, in São José barrio, where twelve families needed a building in which to worship.

What a happy problem!

Just Say No

It was the middle of May 1988. What a month! The DeMerchants had just sent another twenty-five students by boat for Belém. From there the students would travel by bus on to Rio, a four- or five-day-and-night trip. That day was also memorable in that they closed the rental contract for the Rio Negro Gymnasium for their 1988 Crusade in September. In Manaus three new congregations needed buildings. In one service in the church in Coroado barrio, forty-two sinners and backsliders filled the altar.

To top everything, Robert Norris kept urging Bennie to take over the job of national superintendent. To Bennie, that would be like hopping out of the frying pan into the fire to troubleshoot the whole country. In anticipation of the growth throughout Amazonas State, the DeMerchants favored a second Brazilian ABI based in Manaus and were working to that end. In fact, a third Bible school could be built in the northeast of Brazil, perhaps in Recife or Natal.

"In ten years there could be 500 students and by His grace we could seriously work this country over from top to bottom," Bennie wrote to Gerald. However, cultural problems arose because of the different cultures of the people in the North (Amazonas State) and South (Rio). The jungle town man in a huge city must adapt to the type of food, sleeping arrangements (beds versus hammocks), climate, and worship styles. The DeMerchants loathed doing anything that would negatively affect the Bible school in Rio.

"You will not find a finer, better trained, more experienced man than Robert Norris for Bible school work," was Bennie's opinion. "He has high principles and character and is fair, but by being appointed as regional field superintendent (RFS), he just is not around Brazil enough, and when the Foreign Missionary Department had a need for a RFS, they picked the best for their needs, but not for the needs of Brazil."

The needs of their own family had lessened. Beth had married George Sievers, Pam was due to arrive in Manaus under the Associates in Missions (AIM) program after her first year at ABI in St. Paul, and Bennie Joe was growing up faster than the DeMerchants wanted. If Bennie had to go somewhere and couldn't take BJ, the boy howled. BJ had a computer program for IFR and other VFR practice flights and had caught on to landing the plane.

The DeMerchants were expecting missionary Roger Barcus from Grenada to visit them after his retreat in Venezuela. Bennie planned to take Brother Barcus with him when he flew to visit services in some interior towns. He also intended to tease him a bit about his strong faith and making oceanic flights on empty fuel tanks. Brother Barcus had a small wheel plane of his own that he used in the Windward Islands of the Caribbean. One day he was island hopping with his son Jonathan. The radio station on St. Vincent was off the air and he mistook a signal from another station as the one on St. Vincent. Even though off course by just a few degrees, they ended up flying out to sea without enough fuel to find their way back to land. The plane eventually ran out of gas and the engine quit over the Caribbean. Brother Barcus prayed and he felt

God impress him to alter his course. Shortly thereafter he spotted a small sailboat and was able to maneuver the plane just ahead of the craft. A couple was enjoying an oceanic junket and they plucked the intrepid pilot and his son from the ocean shortly after the aircraft slid beneath the waves!

In starting a new work with eager, well-trained students, Bennie and the District Board first looked for towns in areas that needed them and had a good chance to grow. The students had to go there first, try to get a humble place to live, and find a job or something to sell to support themselves. They were not asked to try to get a church going, but to make friends and get contacts with tracts and Search for Truth courses they could start in various homes. When the workers had eight or ten families going well, Bennie and the Board suggested their group rent some small hall somewhere for general meetings. Then they could check with the mayor to see about getting a piece of land.

The UPCB eyed some very good towns on several rivers in which they longed to see churches established. From these key towns where two or three rivers met, a work could be planted. As a church developed, it could reach up and down those rivers into other areas. Inflation, a major, chronic financial problem in Brazil, was running at 30 percent per month: this affected the workers' ability even to subsist.

With the building fund running low, Bennie was happy to get a call from FUNAI to fly 230 kilograms of medicine into three places. After weighing the medicine, he stacked it to the ceiling of the 172; then he cut back on fuel so he could take all the medicine they needed. One place had sixty-five known people with malaria and one person died the day he landed. Four people needed more advanced medical help but Bennie could take only the two sickest.

The nurse, the missionaries, and the Indian chief divided up the medicine, but they almost fought to keep it all in one place.

In spite of the money crunch, the UPCB built several new churches: in Urucará, 150 miles east; Campinas, 90 miles west; Terra Preta, 50 miles west; Pauini, 600 miles southwest; Cruzeiro do Sul, 1,000 miles west-southwest; and three others in Manaus. Bennie wrote the governor of the state to ask for help in getting a piece of land from the government's land distribution center in one of the new suburbs of Manaus. A young couple there had a severely overcrowded church. Bennie hoped the governor could get them a piece of property big enough to accommodate both a parsonage and a church that would seat at least five hundred people.

Many people swarmed to the city for a better education for their family and usually ended up in one of the new areas cut from the jungle that before long turned into a suburb when water and electricity were extended. Bennie also sent a brochure of their last Crusade to the governor and asked if he could break the protocol in their land lot sizes and allow them a lot four times the normal size. If so they would be glad to have the governor visit their Crusade on a Saturday night and greet the people.

The sixteen churches in Manaus and suburbs with their pastors provided the DeMerchants with some wonderful folks. Those great people included fifty student/preachers graduating that year and 140 ministers and lay ministers working in the district. That year their September Crusade would mark twenty-five years since the DeMerchants had been appointed as missionaries to Brazil in San Antonio, Texas, and they felt it would be well attended.

The DeMerchants deeply appreciated the hard-working pastors of the many churches in Manaus, so they invited all the ministers and their wives who pastored a church in Manaus to a barbecue restaurant. Gathered together, they could draw up plans and schedules without driving all over the city for half a day. Bennie wanted to honor these families for the tremendous contribution they made to the work in the city. During the dinner he asked the men to donate some preaching time at some of the interior churches. He felt it was important not only to honor the ministry in a ministerial meeting, but also in front of their various congregations so they would be highly respected. The ministers enjoyed the informal meeting and suggested it be a monthly occurrence!

A diligent young couple from the Rio ABI was getting a group together to buy three lots in downtown Boca do Acre. With the difficult money situation, property was going cheap, but even so the $2,000 price tag was well beyond their means. So the saints in that small church started to pray. God answered in a roundabout way.

Bennie had planned a circuit trip in that area but a sawmill wanted him to deliver a propeller for a tugboat so it could pull a boom of logs in high water to Manaus. The sawmill would pay Bennie about $1,500 to fly men and the propeller to the area and bring the men back. It happened that the men would spend the night on the tugboat in hammocks while Bennie would go to town, buy gas, preach, spend the night, and buy the lots the next day.

"No one but no one would charter a plane to go to a place like that," Bennie observed. "I told the saints that it would be difficult to get these three downtown lots on our tight budget. They just went ahead anyway and prayed it in. The job helped pay for those lots."

A newly acquired computer eased the burden of communicating with the missionaries, the Bible school students, and the now 146 preachers in Amazonas State. Bennie included in his monthly letters a little sermon, a history of what was going on, a nudge to keep working, and plans for the future.

The future looked bright. Bennie had divided the ministers' seminars in the district into three sections: Amazonas East, West, and Central. Those trained men carried the ball of revival in the district, and Bennie felt it was worth all they had ever done to see the work reach that stage. He felt that things would accelerate fast from there on if they could keep the ministers loving each other and working together. They responded positively to challenges. The DeMerchants knew they would be spending eternity with some of the finest people on earth . . . the Amazonians.

On July 15, 1989, Bennie celebrated the thirtieth anniversary of his first solo flight and close to ten thousand hours of total flying time. While in Brazil, he had worn out ten airplane engines. What incidents, accidents, blinding lightning storms, night flights, breakdowns, fuel logistic problems, maintenance, part replacements, and hangar problems he had overcome by a strong conviction of a call from God, hard work, and prayer!

Then that which he had feared came upon him. The National Board elected him as field superintendent of Brazil. He had always looked on that as taking out membership in More Work, Incorporated. He really and truly did not want the job. Sensing, however, that taking the field superintendent's job was the will of God, he couldn't say no.

So he took the job.

The DeMerchant family, circa 1982

Building churches

Flying with the High Fliers

Between the National Board, the current circumstances, and the urging of the Holy Ghost, Bennie accepted the job of field superintendent of Brazil. He realized and deeply appreciated that Brothers Samuel Baker and Robert Norris had worked long and hard to lay a foundation in preaching, teaching, organizing, and training workers in the infancy of the work in Brazil. He did, however, have a great concern.

"Only the good Lord has allowed me to be in this position to do His work and have a means to keep up growth in finance via charter jobs," he explained to Gerald. "With all this extra responsibility on me now, I will not have much time, if any, left over to level up money accounts by flying."

Bennie saw his only alternative was to use the best pastors who had strong, self-supporting churches in Manaus and send them on commercial airlines to preach some meetings in the South. He longed for some new missionaries with a long-term calling who would come, learn the language, and work in one of the Bible schools, two of which were still nonexistent! He had some ideas for practical classes that included digging a foundation, making both cement and ventilated wall blocks by hand, basic bricklaying, wiring, pew-making, plumbing, flooring—in other words the whole ball of wax. He wanted the students to learn how to do business on a small scale to support themselves, such as opening up a sandwich/hot dog stand or coffee shop providing simple meals. The students would also need to learn how to make good contacts and solve people problems.

Bennie thought the students should know how to make charcoal because everyone bought charcoal. One brother made mounds of that every week and sold it by the truckload. Another man ran a chicken farm. Although that was hard work, it turned back small investments quickly with eggs and fried chicken sales. Young students should be learning how to do some of these things to support themselves in new works later on.

The first letter that Bennie wrote in his new job was to Brother and Sister E. J. McClintock at headquarters in St. Louis. At that time, Brother McClintock was Sunday School director for the UPC. Bennie expressed his concern this way: "It is vital to get our Sunday school going. We are losing a high rate of second-generation Pentecostals because of a lack of Sunday school training."

Part of the problem was a dearth of Sunday school materials in the Portuguese language. Brazil had swarms of young people in the churches, but there were no Sunday schools to teach them the Word of God in age-appropriate stories, activities, and games. Bennie promised Brother McClintock that during his visit to Brazil, the focus would be on Sunday school on the two Saturdays and Sundays in the Manacapuru and Manaus areas where together they had about twenty-five to thirty local churches, each of which could handle six hundred people or more. These churches were ripe for Sunday school training.

Pamela, home for the summer under the AIM program, could help with Sunday school training. She brought with her a classmate from ABI, Rosalee Peever. The two young women worked in three of the local churches, giving two-night seminars on evangelism and prayer. Manacapuru, fifty miles upstream from Manaus, had four churches in town and asked Pam to teach Sunday school classes and to speak on the Sunday radio program and in the Sunday night service. The Portuguese language came easily for Pam because she had been born and brought up among the Amazonians.

Of course, with so many blessings being poured on them, Satan had to get in some of his digs. Thieves stole their old '81 SFC diesel pickup from right in front of their house. That was the first time a vehicle had been taken from there. The DeMerchants ran several ads in newspapers describing the truck but got no leads. Remembering all the repairs he had put into it to keep it going, Bennie had mixed emotions to see it gone. However, it had some value and had helped them in hauling building materials for churches around Manaus and loading barges or boats with cement for church construction up the river. The UPCI had pool insurance for all overseas vehicles and they carried only liability insurance locally, but they were trying their best to recover the useful vehicle.

Bennie said later that it must've been the will of God for someone to steal that old pickup. It was always breaking down or out of fuel after being borrowed by a good-but-broke pastor, and Bennie used a lot of time hauling materials and supplies. Finally he hired a man in one of their churches to do those necessary errands, freeing up his own time.

In spite of the additional responsibilities he had taken on, Bennie added another one to his monthly obligations. The mission was now publishing a national newspaper, something Bennie had wanted for years. It provided an excellent way for the people in the Manaus church to see what was happening on the other side of their nation. It boosted morale. The people enjoyed it and the pictures in it. Bennie wrote a lot of the articles and reports for it and bought a couple hundred copies to put into his circular mailouts.

Bennie wrote about and included pictures of church dedications and other activities. He also included statistics of every church reporting from every district of Brazil of their church movement during the past year. Every month they printed five thousand copies.

"With the newspaper plus circulars to the ministry and PIM letters going out bimonthly, we can keep the computer warm," Bennie mentioned to Gerald. "It took a long time to type in all the computer files and keep them upgraded, but I can pull off over three hundred address labels and have the maid stick labels on envelopes and stuff the copies. Keeping in touch with everyone makes coordination much easier."

Shortly afterward, the governor of Amazonas asked Bennie to take him upriver to their floating motorized palace, which had already been sent ahead two days earlier. The governor wanted to fish and hunt ducks over the year-end holidays and come back on January 5. He had just gotten in from Brasilia at the airport after the festivities of his man's winning the presidency of Brazil that week. For reasons of security Bennie couldn't pick him up on the waterfront downtown, so the security guard chose a more isolated and controllable area. The governor with his security men and three others plus their baggage were stuffed into the 206.

The governor sat on the copilot side in front and asked questions about where they were. For smoother flying, Bennie climbed on top of a scattered overcast, and a glimpse down a hole in the clouds now and then told him where he was. He preferred that to flying lower or through the overcast and getting someone's stomach rolling more than necessary. An hour and twenty minutes out from Manaus, Bennie eased back and dropped down through the overcast with the designated lake over the nose of the plane. He spotted their boat way up ahead behind the trees and dropped in on a straight line, stopping at the back of the boat with a step on a platform for climbing up inside.

"The governor now wants to go to North America to get them a floatplane rather than all the expensive hardware they have that has to stick to airports," Bennie revealed to Gerald.

Although Bennie had folded-up charts tucked away close at hand, he smiled to himself when he heard the governor comment to some of the staff that they had come straight to the boat without a chart. "I suppose after flying ten thousand hours here, one is permitted to show off a little," Bennie remarked to Gerald.

The governor invited Bennie to eat with them inside their palatial yacht in the dining room section. They had everything on the table and big salads that no one touched, all right there in the middle of the jungle. He sat Bennie beside him and while eating asked if Bennie knew of a better place to catch bass. Bennie did, of course! He indicated a much better place only half the distance from Manaus that held bigger fish in clearer water. Then Bennie pulled out four new Mickey Finn lures that he donated to the governor and told him how to use them.

It seems that everyone has a hairy dog story and Bennie has his. On a long, quiet Easter weekend when no boats plied the river and few if any buses rolled through the streets, Bennie decided to drive to the lake and cross to the hangar. Their old German shepherd dog, Pepsi, had two younger dogs to train to protect the property. She loved to go with Bennie in the pickup truck to the hangar. She would dive from the water taxi boat with no urging and would swim a mile a day on her own. Bennie had never seen a dog that liked the water more than Pepsi. Some of the natives fondly claimed her family tree had an alligator in it whose genes had come on strong.

The taxi canoe left the floating hangar to return Bennie across two hundred yards of water to the pickup at twilight. As usual, old Pepsi dived in, swimming around in the water and barking for the other dogs to follow. Rain, just starting, brought in a very low ceiling that set in fast. After circling a point of land, the canoe taxi turned right; beyond at the left some good-sized log booms encircled a sawmill. The little dogs swam faster than Pepsi and splashed out of the water as Bennie unhooked the pickup. He chatted with some people wanting a ride to town, but no Pepsi appeared. Bennie called and waited half an hour until darkness rolled in with the rain in full force. Bennie had a District Board meeting waiting and thought to pick Pepsi up the next morning and swing past the floating hangar where she sometimes spent the night.

When Bennie got home with no Pepsi, the girls were pretty cross. The maid and the secretary loved the old dog. So from then on until Saturday Bennie drove around that area but no one knew where the old dog was. Bennie kind of wrote her off but the girls wanted to take the Bug and look for her. Of course, BJ begged to go with them.

At last Bennie agreed on driving the girls around the area once more. They would have to drive to the barrio of Aleixo and go in a canoe taxi around the bend of the lake arm to the floating hangar. Three or four hills met the lake there, and checking with all the people who lived near the water would take time.

The girls and BJ had squeezed into the Bug when the phone rang. Emergency! An old man in Autazes had fallen from his ladder while fixing a roof. Badly hurt and bleeding internally, he needed an airlift to Manaus. Immediately.

Bennie groaned. Even if all went well it would be tough to drive to the hangar, gas up the plane, take out the seats, and hop the river to Autazes. He was strongly tempted to say that it was impossible. Chances were the old fellow would not live till the next day. Then Bennie recalled a night several years earlier, when he and Brother Upton had spent the evening with him and his wife explaining baptism in Jesus' name. With their own Bible open, they read the Scriptures and saw the truth. Bennie baptized them that night beside the floats of the 172.

The kids howled their disappointment that they were not going to look for Pepsi and bring her back to the house. Reluctantly they crawled out of the Bug. Bennie promised he'd take them to find Pepsi as soon as he could.

Airlifting the old man to Manaus would have to be a quick trip and Bennie knew there was no use thinking of any reimbursement. He told the caller to get the old man to a ramp in front of the city where the water meets it and wait till he arrived.

After the thirty-minute hop to Autazes, Bennie and a couple of family members lifted the injured man up to the floor of the airplane. The poor fellow moaned and groaned in pain. His family members scrambled inside to hold his head and comfort him. Bennie taxied out into the current away from the boats and took off. With lights of the suburb reflecting on the water, Bennie splashed down and taxied directly to where he'd left his pickup truck. Other family members had their car ready to receive Grandpa to rush him to the hospital.

Bennie helped remove the injured fellow from the plane and into car. As Bennie turned to reenter the plane, the man's son stopped him.

"What is your charge?" the younger man asked. "How much do we owe you?"

"I'll just write it on a piece of ice and throw it in the river," Bennie replied.

The son gave Bennie an ear-to-ear smile and a hearty hug before he got in their old noisy car. He floored the gas pedal in first gear to get up over the steep hill and on their way.

After putting the plane away at the floating hangar around the turn in the arm of the lake and hailing a canoe taxi back, it was Bennie's turn to get in his pickup and drive up the hill. So as he shifted into second gear at the top of the hill, Bennie exclaimed out loud alone in the truck, "Lord, I did Your work. Now where's my dog?"

The words had barely left Bennie's mouth when a very assertive man strode into the headlights. He stood right in the middle of the road, spread his legs apart, and raised his hands up in the air like a traffic cop.

Bennie braked the truck and rolled down the window.

The man strode over to the open window and queried, "Pastor, don't you have a German shepherd dog the people see on the back of your pickup truck at times that has been missing a few days?"

"Yes!" Bennie's heart beat a bit faster.

"Well, the other night after the rain hit we were out on the lake setting up our nets. On the way back we flashed our light over a big boom of logs and spotted a black German shepherd dog that looked like she had become very tired swimming among them. We coaxed her to us and pulled her into our canoe and brought her home. We chained her in our garage and fed her. If you come over we will give her back to you."

Wow! Bennie thought. *Praise the Lord! I rarely see God answer a prayer so fast!*

When he got home the girls heard a lesson about doing the right thing first and God will make the rest fall into place. But amidst the happy barking and tail-wagging and dog-hugging, he's not sure how much the kids heard of his lesson!

Bennie claims the dog story proves that God has a sense of humor and sometimes the way the Lord works can blow a person's mind. The DeMerchants weren't smiling a few days later, however. A message from the United States caused great sadness, and events in Brazil brought them disappointment.

Bennie Jonas and increased responsibilities
with more "Pepsis"

Pepsi loved water!

Have Hammock, Will Travel

In 1990, Bennie had flown Brothers James Yohe, Sam Bessler, and William LaRue, visiting ministers from the United States, for a two-week trek far upriver near the Colombian and Peruvian borders. After church service one night in Tabatinga, he received a phone call from Theresa. He knew something was wrong for her to be calling him at that late hour. She told him that Brother S. G. Norris, president of ABI in St. Paul, Minnesota, had died.

Just as he had never forgotten where he was when he heard of the assassination of US President John Kennedy, Bennie would never forget that telephone booth in the hotel in Tabatinga, Brazil, near the Colombian border. He took Theresa's message back to the men who had flown with him a thousand miles west of Manaus to dedicate three new churches, and who were also graduates of "the school we love."

Bennie had just written a letter to Brother Norris in which he remarked that

> ministers are like trees that have all kinds of roots. We had one of our first churches several years ago on an island in the middle of the Amazon River. Near it stood a huge samauma

tree that took about 50 paces to walk around its base, since even its roots were too high to step over. I used it for a landmark. The jungle would be green in every direction. While approaching this church on the island from any direction with the airplane, even 10 miles away on a clear day, I could look ahead, spot that huge tree stuck up above all others, point the nose of the plane toward it and come out by the church. I have often thought of you as that tree with your doctrinal roots near that of the church.

In our early years here when there was no fellowship and finances were slim, on several occasions you would drop us a note of encouragement as well as an unexpected check. Our roots strengthened and we hung on when it seemed like there would never be a church here.

If the Lord tarries and you should be absent from us, you know that your teaching impact will go on and on not only here in Brazil, but in all the world where ABI students work.

As for a Bible school in Manaus, the DeMerchants had to swallow their own hopes, at least for a while. The Franklin Howards, who had been in charge of the ABI in Rio, had returned to the US early to work on reducing their deficit for the school operation and to raise some funds for the new school year starting in April. In order to accommodate the growing number of students, the Rio Bible school had to increase the size of the married couples' dorm and construct a new three-story dorm for singles to hold one hundred students.

"All problems of the national work end up on my phone or in my mailbox," Bennie wrote Gerald. To escape from the clamor of incessant phone calls for a while, Bennie slipped away with BJ in the 172 on a short run for the two of them to be together at the floating lodge. Swinging in his hammock, Bennie enjoyed the blessed silence—silence, that is, if he discounted the flutter of wings of hundreds of vampire bats coming and going through a hole in the roof overhead. Howling from rambunctious monkeys in the trees added to the din.

Like the circuit riders in early American history, Bennie made circuits to as many of the churches that he could as often as he could. When those visits could be paid for by some other agency, Bennie happily gave his service to a project. For example, he used the 206 to ferry Congresswoman Sadie Hauachie and two of her secretaries to visit ten towns in six days as she campaigned for her reelection. Sadie went to the States quite often; she had gone to college in England and had spent four years in France.

Two months before a general congressional election, she decided to meet and greet as many of her constituents as she could. She had prepaid by helping get his airplane imported into Brazil, and to keep his word he gave her the flight hours he would have spent had he returned to the US and back with his airplane. While she took care of her campaign and political encounters with town officials, Bennie was able to meet the mayors of those towns and minister at night in a local church. Bennie visited churches and slept in the homes of his own ministers, who were already penetrating these areas with the gospel message. The good thing was that the time credit he promised her was short, and soon the campaign would be over.

Bennie, being apolitical, hated waiting on a riverbank while Sadie was campaigning. Never able to be idle, he took his books and magazines and wrote articles for their national paper. He had a flashlight and a battery-operated electric portable typewriter with memory with which to do his own writing projects.

Sadie, however, wasn't the only government official who hired Bennie to fly her throughout her district. The state government and state and federal congressmen, citing Bennie's willingness to fly Sadie around, pressured him to fly them into various places so they could ride on her coattails.

At one time, for a period of eight to ten years in Manaus, Bennie was actually the only one with a small plane licensed and up to date airworthy-wise to fly in and out of narrow places with only water as the airport. Once when Bennie was at São Paulo de Olivença on the Solimões River, a high drug area, a judge begged Bennie to fly him back to Manaus, a seven-hour flight.

A crowd had gathered on the riverbank as the judge approached with someone else carrying his suitcase. To the judge's surprise, Bennie stopped them before getting in the plane and quietly asked him to open that suitcase. The people on the river edge looked on while their judge obliged.

Later, in flight, the judge asked why Bennie had wanted the suitcase opened.

"This is a high drug traffic area," Bennie responded, "and I do not know you. If anything is asked of me, I want to be able to respond to any accusation that I had the passenger who was not one of my pastors open his suitcase so I could verify the contents of it since I was giving him a ride with me back to Manaus."

"You are very right, pastor," the judge answered. "We all trust you and your mission greatly."

In another adventure, Bennie took a judge with a fear of flying way up the Japurá River to Vila Bitencourt. The mayor of Coari, who helped their constituency so much at conference time, had asked the judge to investigate reports of electoral fraud. The judge's visit would surprise everyone in this remote Brazilian town on the Colombian border. He would examine the sealed ballot boxes and decide if the seal had been violated before arriving by boat in Manaus.

From the time Bennie whirled the propeller to start the engine to taxi for takeoff on the Solimões River, he explained every function of the plane and how it all worked. The judge became so interested and relaxed that he enjoyed the flight. To Bennie's surprise on returning to Manaus, the judge told him that he was the only person who had been able to relieve his fear of flying. The judge later actually enjoyed his long jet trips to southern Brazil.

Later, after the judge had been transferred to Manaus, the computer pulled his name to preside over a law case that involved the UPCB. A rebellious pastor who had fallen in sin was giving the church leaders fits in Manaus and refused to budge from their building. The church prayed hard for help. Bennie believes there were about nineteen judges at the time of the trial, and the computer chose the one who had flown with him and who knew him! Bennie felt it was the hand of God. The judge told Bennie's lawyer that when he saw Bennie's name and signature on the document, he was not even going to read it because he knew that Bennie Leigh DeMerchant would give him what he was asking for in the process. The UPCB won the case. Bennie won six other cases brought against the church. He attributed that to the goodwill he established while flying judges and legislators, mayors and governors of Amazonas State around.

Using the planes demanded that they be maintained, so Bennie hired a good aircraft mechanic to work part time with him at the hangar to keep the "birds" safe and in order. They would chain the propellers and throttle locks with padlocks on each plane at the hangar because drug dealers usually ran off with the best plane they could find in any area. Too many little things kept eating up Bennie's time, so he trusted those errands to the mechanic to run them in his car. Aircraft mechanics have credentials from Brazilian Aeronautics and work for maintenance companies also credentialed for giving inspections for every 50, 100, 200, 500, and 1,000 hours of flight. They know all the common defects on engines, aircraft cells and propellers, and sign off every annual inspection in all three aircraft log books. They comply with the factory updates on any bugs in a component of their aircraft with owners worldwide.

Bennie's caretaker at the floating hangar got lazy and wouldn't even cut the grass. After going there three times and finding the place abandoned, Bennie installed another family who started a church nearby that in a year grew to eighty members. Bennie let him live at his house near the hangar and take care of the church.

Sometimes Bennie maintained the plane himself. He had the 206 in the floating hangar on dry dock, fixing a right float bottom that had recently landed in low water and scraped a pointed rock in the shadows just as the plane was falling off the step to taxi. Bennie had cringed at the sound of aluminum grating over rock. He had carefully studied the landing from air passes and it looked okay, but with black water, dark rocks, shade from overhanging trees, and very little current to make a telltale eddy, a rock lurking just under the surface at the end of the pool stabbed the pontoon.

The pontoons, also called floats, have seven compartments each for safety. If one is punctured, water only partially enters inside of it, and though the pontoon is even lower in the water, the other compartments support the weight. However, the leaking or punctured compartment needs to be pumped out before takeoff. They stuffed a sock in the hole with the point of a screwdriver, bailed the water out, and ran for the air. Bennie liked adventure if it was low risk but not the kind that damages a float. Once arriving at home base in Manaus, the plane would have to be dry docked and one side held up by fuel drums while the pontoon was removed and taken to a local maintenance division where a professional riveter would replace the damaged aluminum and return it to service.

Shortly after their return to Manaus after their deputation in the early '90s, the DeMerchants, in concurrence with the national board, approved a new national church flag and national anthem for the UPC of Brazil to be sung at their main functions. They eagerly looked forward to reestablishing their local training program and to opening the Rio Bible school again as well.

Philip Walmer, a missionary in Porto Alegre, had revised all of their tracts and was printing three new very-much-needed books. He had also done an excellent job translating David K. Bernard's book *In Search of Holiness* into Portuguese. By computer Bennie mailed out about 350 of the books to their ministry, feeling that was the best investment in helping their people and ministry maintain some kind of a moderate stand and give direction to those where they were unable to minister in person.

They also started the Faith Promise plan among the current Manaus churches. They had $4,000 per month pledged but were aiming for $6,000. The DeMerchants pressed the need to see souls saved, and tried to plant a missions attitude of helping others among their people. They noticed that the lower middle class had begun attending their churches more now. Some small businessmen who drove fairly good used cars had become members. They were glad to see people of a higher education and income level, some of whom were college students or even graduates, attending various churches. In the early years

147

Bennie's new Jeep had been the only vehicle in front of the church. With the blessings of God on them, he often had to hunt for two blocks to find a parking place in front of ABI. He had to leave his house early to find a parking spot inside Jerusalem Conference Center or else be trapped outside by the many buses, vehicles, motorcycles, and boats that came to this place for evening services.

To encourage the Faith Promise plan, Bennie had one thousand PIM certificates printed on a golden background that they wanted to have on hand at the churches when missionary appointees presented their burden. In addition, the DeMerchants wanted to get some missionary maps that included pictures of the missionaries. The ultimate twofold goal was to put new men into unchurched states in the Amazon and to send Brazilian missionaries to Portuguese-speaking countries abroad that had no missionaries at the time. Although they received requests from abroad for missionaries, at that time they had none available nor did they have any structure for their support and operation.

The DeMerchants understood that growth required a solid, deep foundation. So, in typical full throttle mode of operation, they began to dig one.

Robert and Jean Norris

Jack Leaman in the Amazon, with Bennie

Ivana Norris and Theresa DeMerchant

The late Reverend and Sister S. G. Norris

Making Waves

In a flurry of feverish activity, Bennie, the pastors, and the workers in Manaus finished the work on the new central church building just in time for the Manaus Crusade. The attendance increased each night by about five hundred people, and on the closing night of the crusade, thirty-two hundred people filled the galleries and most of the seats on the main floor. Many of their own people couldn't come because their flimsy houses needed protection from thieves. That meant visitors filled half of the seats. In addition to the great attendance, the Lord gave them three cool days.

During the crusade they distributed slips to the visitors and asked them to fill in their name and address and indicate if they wanted prayer for healing, a visit in their home to discuss a problem, or if they were interested in having an informal Bible study course taught in their home. In all, seven hundred slips were turned in, and the pastors of each area of Manaus played post office and separated each one to the nearest church of the ten in Manaus. The pastors floated around on cloud nine in anticipation of making these new contacts. Needless to say, the pastors were very enthusiastic about having another crusade!

After the crusade, the DeMerchants hosted an

International Youth Crusade (IYC) led by Terry Pugh. While the IYC was in Manaus, Bennie responded to several emergency calls early in the day while the young people were resting in a hotel in central Manaus or recuperating or shopping. Brother Pugh went with him in the 206 to get a snake-bitten Indian boy who was carried in a hammock from a huge, round, thatch-roofed house to the plane. Then he rescued a family of Americans ridden with malaria out of an Indian tribe that the MAF (Missionary Aviation Fellowship) couldn't touch because their operation used wheeled planes. On another morning he took off with the 172 before daylight to get a small, young, Indian woman with a half-born baby that had been dead for seventy hours. Bennie was able to take her to an ambulance at the ferry crossing near the floating hangar. Later he was glad to learn that the young woman was going to be all right. Before these emergency flights ended, Bennie plucked a man out of the Atroaris who had severed a vein in his arm and had lost a lot of blood.

Bennie wondered who would be doing rescue work while they were away on their next furlough. Wycliffe had sold their old 206 on floats several years earlier; the Adventist pilot was away; and the Mid-Missions people had crashed their plane. The only group left was having document problems. In the middle of all this activity, Bennie was trying hard to finish up the thirtieth church.

"Our cash flow looks like the reversing falls with the tide out, but I just had to get some things wound up before furlough and went ahead on my own," Bennie wrote Gerald. "We have new churches bulging with the roof scarcely on. During this term we spent about $125,000 in building funds for these 30 churches, 20 of them built of cement blocks. I love to stretch our dollars on exchange, finance with no interest on Brazilian money when possible, and get all the help from the local congregations to at least buy a lot and donate their labor to erect the shell of a building."

At the end of June, Bennie wrote Gerald that their itinerary on this furlough would cover mostly the eastern half of the United States. They still did not know who was coming to supervise the work. In spite of that concern, the DeMerchants eagerly anticipated having the month of August off for a vacation—with pay! They toyed with the idea of taking the kids to Disney World and then either boarding a night flight from Orlando or riding the Amtrak to St. Louis, for something different for the kids.

When they returned to Brazil a year later, Bennie observed that when he had started flying there years ago, some of the isolated towns in the interior didn't even have communication with Manaus by radio, but now had direct dialing via satellite. One could see so many paradoxes here in Brazil! For example, a person might see a horse and buggy bringing a barrel of aviation fuel from the pastor's house in Parintins to the 206 floatplane a few hundred yards away.

The chaotic Brazilian economy adversely affected the DeMerchants. The country, though democratic, was riddled by shortages, and a black market existed for nearly everything. While the DeMerchants had been on deputation in the US, the Brazilian government chopped three zeros off the money and started a new currency. At the same time, they froze basic commodity and food prices and those on fuel, transportation tickets, and vehicles. They held down the cost of cars, but all the car agencies were sold out. Airlines were overloaded, and though ticket prices were much reduced, there was no seating space. In São Paulo, commuter airlines had a load factor for the Air Bridge to Rio averaging 95 percent; fights broke out for seats at the gates.

Although the government taxed gasoline and subsidized diesel fuel, the price of aviation gas had been tabled and held down to steady transportation costs. Bennie could buy a fifty-five gallon barrel of aviation gas for fifty-two dollars. He expected the price to blow any day, but he had all his barrels full, with forty-nine of them scattered throughout the state and about thirty barrels in the garage and hangar in Manaus. Inflation in the Brazilian economy was over 1,000 percent. In the month of June alone, it was nearly 29 percent—1 percent per day in Brazilian currency. The poor people with fixed salaries had it rough. Bennie was awed when he saw such poor people pay their tithes; he knew they were truly sacrificing.

One day he decided to take two air traffic controllers to a nearby lake for some fishing. He had in mind a clean cow pasture that edged the black water that indicated lurking bass. The controller flew the 206 from the right side. Sitting there, the man was exposed to a new world of information because he saw what happened inside the cabin: the radio, speed, attitude, direction, and altitude.

They skied to a stop by the cow pasture and tied up to a stump. Bennie got out three fly rods and put new leaders and new tucunaré special flies on each. His companions walked around with him and beat and thrashed those lines trying to reach out where Bennie naturally threw them. Before long, Bennie was pulling in fish and his friends had their lines in knots and the hooks full of grass from their back casts. Bennie quickly caught a six pounder, then gave it to one of the other men, untangled the man's line and hooked a fish for him. Then he did the same thing for the second fellow. Two hours later they took off for home and Bennie left them at their front gates with a plastic bag full of fish. Now when Lima Echo Echo flew, those men in the tower had an idea of where Bennie's home base lake was in relation to the airport traffic at both the old and new airports.

Bennie and Theresa were up to their ears with the work. The DeMerchants saw their more experienced men maturing. These men respected the missionaries and worked well with the less experienced workers who were coming up. As busy as the DeMerchants were, they saw the need for a work in Cruzeiro do Sul in the state of Acre, a very fine city with a population of one hundred thousand up the Juruá River two hours flight time beyond Eirunepé. This good-sized town had two direct jet flights a week from Manaus, but it was so far out that few missions thought of going there.

All the churches and pastors sent their tithes to the district treasury. These funds were used for district expenses, for renting buildings, opening up new works, and for evangelism. Some of these funds were used to send the pastor of the largest church in Manaus to a new place in Acre to open up a work. Mister Abraham, a local Manaus man, owned a huge supermarket in Manaus. He also owned various tugboats and barges. Bennie had helped him when the diesel tugboat needed a new part and Bennie was able to get the boat operating again in a few hours. He told Bennie not to worry about land for a church or sending freight, cement blocks, or aviation gas since he would put anything they wanted on a barge in Manaus and transport the materials to the new work for free. Not only that, but Mr. Abraham ran his barges east to Belém.

"We think this is an open door, even if it takes two months of pushing the barge to get there," Bennie wrote Gerald.

Another place ripe for the gospel was Boca do Acre, a fine town at the junction of the Acre and Purús Rivers. This would serve as an opening town for other cities farther up that river, a converging point just two days by boat above the present church in Pauini, and would be good for fellowship with that church. A fine young ABI-trained couple had a thriving church there. The DeMerchants were impressed by the quality and training of the graduates from the ABI in Rio.

"They are really cutting the mustard," Bennie wrote to Gerald. "Every week they are bringing in souls and baptizing people in some areas to the point where the pastor hardly dares leave town for lack of help."

In Coari, the pastor practically took over a small interior Catholic community and baptized ten to fifteen people a week who were also praying through. Disturbed, the priest and a seminary student visited the pastor to question why those folks left the Roman Catholic Church. Later, some testified that the priest smoked one cigarette after another. He couldn't refute a word but left in a huff. The kids of the schoolteachers in their church had first got saved and then worked in an area holding house meetings. By the time the priest got word of what was going on, it was too late. Another denomination printed an article written by their district superintendent about the great danger that "monotheism" was posing to their work in the region. The DeMerchants just chuckled at that one!

The DeMerchants were also planning the Manaus Missionary Retreat for all of the South American missionaries. To accommodate the missionaries and all of the congregations in Manaus, the district rented the Rio Negro Sports Club auditorium, which would seat up to four thousand people.

Since the earlier crusade, the churches in Manaus had been blessed with new people, including the central church with about twenty new converts. Some students out of another organization's seminary were baptized in Jesus' name. The pastor who had gone to Cruzeiro do Sul with four workers about seven months earlier now had close to a hundred believers who were stirring the town. Another organization had had three crusades since the one Bennie organized in Manaus, but they went flat and dead even with politicians present. Outsiders told the DeMerchants their crusade was the best.

During the month of October, Bennie had been seated behind a whirling propeller one hundred hours in forty days. FUNAI had him making a number of runs. An epidemic broke out among the Atroari in the Comanaú and Alalaú River areas. Six or so died of malaria or German measles. On one trip of over an hour, an Indian was carried to the plane and drank water in his cupped hands just before settling in the seat in the 206 behind Bennie. Although weak, the Indian seemed to know what was going on, but he died ten minutes before landing in Manaus in front of an awaiting ambulance that had been radioed for ahead of time. Brother Ellis from Canton, Ohio, was with Bennie on that flight, and it shook him up to see that weak, bony old man die so helplessly.

On another trip, a woman died in childbirth just before Bennie arrived at the outpost, and they were putting out the candles when he got there. Another died after his arrival but fortunately many more were restored to health after being flown to FUNAI's House for Indians in Manaus. There medical people attended to the sick, and sometimes these persons returned with him to their original tribe in good health.

Since one of the other pilots that FUNAI used had quit, the government continued to use Bennie's services. Bennie did not think of himself as a celebrity, but when it came right down to it, his and Theresa's was one of the very few mission-owned floatplanes in the entire Amazon basin, and at times the only one that operated on water with access to remote places inaccessible to all the others.

Sometimes when new pilots were imported to Manaus they could fly electronically by radio navigation using instruments. Bennie, however, held a big advantage. With thousands of hours of visual flying out of Manaus as a hub and like spokes of a wheel going out in all directions, the knowledge of the area, rivers, islands, tributaries, lakes, and backwaters was engraved in his memory. Even in rain or marginal visual conditions with intermittent rain and low cloud ceilings, in a quick glance, Bennie knew where he was and in which direction to look for the next reference on the trip. That distant puddle of water twenty miles or more away indicated a natural airport in that direction.

As one military pilot, who had been transferred from southern Brazil to fly military planes or helicopters, explained to Bennie, none of them got the chance to acquire the experience he had received from his long flights in the "air turtle" on these rivers and highlands near the end of the watershed on the neighboring countries' borders where many of the Indian tribes lived, each tribe able to call for help on their two-way radio.

However, the next call came not from FUNAI, but from two Wycliffe Bible Translator missionaries to the Maku Indian tribe near the town of Barcelos on the huge, almost uninhabited Negro River. Because of the drizzling rain beating on the window of the Cessna 206, he flew low, close to the riverbank. In bad weather he had developed his own IFR (I Follow River) habit, knowing that a natural airport was always below the pontoons.

Two hours northwest of Manaus through a moderate rain, Bennie needed to land to transfer fuel from three six-gallon jerricans in the baggage compartment in the floats to the wing tank. That would add to his range for the rainy season's unpredictable changes in weather. He glanced at the engine oil pressure gauge. Its indicator needle slanted low on the green arc. In seconds it dropped lower and flickered off the green. Bennie stared in unbelief at the extremely low reading on his oil pressure gauge. He hovered above a finger-like backwater lake that looked big enough to land on, so he taxied up to its white sandy beach and checked the oil. The oil level was off the end of the stick! Bennie poured in all his quarts of reserve oil to bring the gauge back up to a safe flying level.

On this deserted lake, Bennie and his two passengers were isolated from river traffic. He skipped the plane to the main river, searching for a place to land. Soon he spotted two small thatch-roofed houses on the left bank of the river below. A small diesel-powered boat was tied up in front of the house. He cut power and landed again.

Bennie and his passengers stepped off the pontoons of the plane onto the shore. The bottom of the floatplane was black with oil from the engine to the tail! Oil dripped off into the river, making a long slick in the current. Then he pulled the oil measuring dipstick, holding his breath. No oil in the engine crank case touched the bottom of the stick!

Bennie removed the hood of the engine and washed all the black oil off with airplane gasoline. He idled the engine a few seconds and discovered the culprit—a leaking oil radiator with a fine hairline crack at its base. The oil cooler behind the propeller had a broken support and under pressure, oil spurted out.

The men prayed. The two young passengers held the SSB radio antenna as high as possible on a long pole while a man barked out in Portuguese, "This is an emergency!" to a mission frequency in Porto Velho in southern Brazil. The signal faded in and out. They kept calling their home base six hundred miles to the south, giving the part number of what was needed. They also asked for more oil and tools to work with. A Missionary Aviation Fellowship (MAF) plane picked up the signal and forwarded it to the Wycliffe base in Porto Velho. They gave the attendants at Porto Velho the oil cooler make, model, and serial number. The personnel there contacted their engine overhaul shop in southern Brazil, which located a new Harrison oil radiator that would fit Bennie's 300-horsepower Continental engine in São Paulo.

Then an amazing Amazon relay began. The next passenger jet flight north flew the radiator to Porto Velho. There a waiting Wycliffe JARS (Jungle Aviation and Radio Services) pilot transported the radiator, a case of oil, and tools to the little village airport of Barcelos the next day.

In the meantime Bennie and the others rented the small, leaky boat from the homeowners to take them in the wind and rain six hours upriver to Barcelos. The woman and children (somewhat awed by that colorful flying machine) stayed behind with the plane tied up on the shore in front of the house. The men spent the night at a country hotel while the other wheel plane arrived to their rescue. In the moonlight early on the following morning they returned to the floatplane in the boat. Bennie replaced the oil cooler after sunrise, tested it, and they took off.

They all thanked the Lord for how quickly the problem was solved. They had been down in the back of beyond in the Amazon jungle in the rainy season. They were flying again in forty-eight hours!

Bennie now had the kindness of another mission to reciprocate deeds and flights when one or the other was down or needed parts. Whether Bennie agreed or not with the doctrine preached by others, it was in order to do a helping deed for a friend down in the jungle if he knew of it and had any reasonable power to change the situation. One day, such mutual support would come back with interest in some way, somewhere.

The radio was a valuable tool in the work in Manaus. One of the brethren from the Manaus church had a daily radio program. The man spoke clearly and aggressively, challenging the gainsayers. He painted such vivid word pictures of churches that the listener already knew who they were. He almost dared them to come to a church that believes in real worship and where God could give a person the baptism of the Holy Ghost where they would speak with other tongues. Visitors walked in from off the street or from other churches. In the past two months the man had baptized thirty converts and prayed another thirty through to the Holy Ghost. The radio program cost about twenty dollars each day, but that church became widely known since the program reached with reasonable clarity all of Manaus and about a 150-mile radius on the medium wavelength (MW) band.

And waves of truth lapped farther and farther along the banks of the Amazon and its tributaries.

Pastor Cezar Rener Ferreira, head of ABI, Manaus

A Pile of Gumption

The DeMerchants had long dreamed of having Bible schools in the northern part of Brazil. Over the years they had sent several hundred students to the ABI in Rio de Janeiro, where the students had received sound, thorough training. The zeal and energy of these graduates made tremendous inroads into nearly every region of the country. In 1990, however, the Bible school in Rio closed for three years. When the DeMerchants returned to Manaus at the end of their furlough, they returned to a truly empty nest. Beth had married George Sievers, and Pam was finishing her education in Minnesota. Bennie Joe had lost his eighteen-month battle against cancer, and the house at Rua Ramos Ferreira contained precious, bittersweet memories of the boy who had been his dad's shadow. Bennie had always valued Theresa's worth, but he stood in awe and amazement at the special anointing of grace and power the Lord poured into her after their son's death.

When they got themselves resettled in Manaus, they found that with the temporary closure of the Rio ABI, the young people had been clamoring for a Bible school of their own. The pastors in Manaus responded to their insistence—and elected Theresa to oversee the program!

163

The DeMerchants' dream for a Bible school in Manaus was finally realized in 1993, and in 1994, thirty-four students returned for a second year of study. Eighty-nine eager first-year learners joined them to push the facilities of the central church to its limits. Using her experience and expertise, Theresa hand-picked the teachers from among the Brazilian pastors who had churches in Manaus. They worked with her on all matters, but Theresa closely monitored the teachers, the students, and the curriculum. Manacapuru, never far behind whatever the Manaus church did, also began a Bible school. Before long, the churches in Boa Vista and Maués had opened Bible schools. That gave northern Brazil 172 students in training programs. Many of the schools' teachers had been trained to excellence by Brother Robert Norris or in the school he started in Rio.

A week after the opening of the second year of Bible school operation, Bennie reported to Gerald that the schools were rolling along fine. They had had to turn down eight late students just that week because not only were they out of books, but they were out of room! They soon bought and cleared a lot behind the central church, and they had to build again because the Bible school program was snowballing. They had swarms of youth who saw that they needed training to get ahead.

The DeMerchants knew that some students would drop out after three or four months, but they also knew that school really showed who was who by the students' grades and the seriousness of the studies. They gave them all they could in the two-year, three-nights-a-week course and Theresa screened out seven of the pastors for teachers. With the church packed with students keen to learn, the teachers counted it a great honor to be chosen to teach, and some wanted to teach more than one subject. All the churches in Manaus agreed to hold their meetings on off nights to allow their married men working a job to attend the local church services and still be in class at night and have family life in between. The students got a stack of material to take home during the year. The Xerox copier ran overtime to keep up! It seemed they called a serviceman every week.

The concept of Bible school training expanded to many other states in Brazil until almost eleven hundred students were enrolled. Not all students finished the course, but generally after two years the average class graduated between 55 and 60 percent of its students. Those who finished the two-year Bible school course in Manaus were honored with a graduation ceremony that thousands attended. Bennie flew to other districts and ministered at their graduations or when unable, sent another minister to do so.

The DeMerchants honored Bible school graduates who had good grades to be teachers in other states of Brazil, and wrote many circular letters to hundreds of ministers encouraging them to start a school. The churches exploded with new young people receiving an experience with God and dedicating their lives to His service. These trained young men and women reached out into untouched areas and states, starting more churches and Bible schools until eventually fifty schools peppered Brazil. The DeMerchants chose Bible school teachers who had first graduated with high marks from an ABI school. Then they assisted a teacher in the classroom. After this year of teacher training, the potential teacher could be assigned a class in Manaus or sent to another needy area where small districts wanted to train their youth.

"My mother told me early that my marriage to Theresa was one tremendous choice," Bennie noted. "Theresa's untiring zeal amidst many obstacles and setbacks just keeps on going. She has a pile of gumption from her German background. She adapts readily to difficult situations and with her crew of helpers accomplishes an astonishing amount of work."

As effective as Theresa was in overseeing the Bible schools, one of her greatest joys was praying with people as they sought the Holy Ghost. A Roman Catholic priest ran across some Search for Truth material. The simple designs piqued his curiosity, and he started studying the lessons one by one. Wondering why the central Manaus church was growing so fast, he decided to visit it.

At the end of their services, the pastor called all the people, saint or sinner, to gather around the altar and pray, and the church folk usually brought their guests with them. The priest, Cezar Rener Ferreira, joined the group. The minister explained to outsiders about repenting and believing that God heard and forgave them, so that in faith they could worship and thank God for the gift of the Holy Ghost.

Theresa always loved praying with seekers of this gift and has prayed many, many people through to this great experience in God. After praying awhile, Theresa went to the priest and told him to raise his hands and worship God. She put her hands on his shoulders and suggested repeating about five expressions of praise. Slowly and softly he obeyed her urgings. Then his worship gradually increased till it became louder and louder. The power of God struck him. Speaking in tongues, he bounced like a basketball. Rather than be stomped on, Theresa drew back. The men around tried to keep Brother Cezar from hurting himself and others with the tremendous joy he felt at that time.

What a total transformation in his life! He wrote his bishop and the pope about leaving his vow to the Catholic Church, and was relieved of it. He later married Theresa's ABI secretary, Maria, who had worked for seventeen years with her in the Manaus ABI. The Cezars, with his executive team and teacher pool, now head the Manaus Bible school. They manage the distribution of books by phone orders and mailing to the other 123 ABIs in all of Brazil. He also controls the book stock, keeping an eye on the thirty-six textbooks used in the classes. Any textbook with less than 500 in stock has to be reprinted. To keep the price down, Brother Cezar prints 5,000 books at a time, about 60,000 per year. Brother Cezar coordinates all of the districts in the UPC of Brazil and visits those other districts to check on Bible school operations, problems, needs, and activities.

Satan, of course, tried to sabotage the growing cadre of young people eager to spread the Jesus Name message. He attacked from the flank through a few pastors who developed a mutiny of sorts. Bennie confused the rebels by just sending out a letter to all other ministers in their district to set some things straight. The rebellious leaders' minds were made up, but Bennie confounded them with the facts by proving they had violated the UPCB manual with their privately called meetings of small, selected, invited groups to liberate this or that or take over properties.

"Oh, the power of a computer and printer and Xerox machine and the Post Office!" Bennie wrote Gerald. "I imagine Paul would have envied the twentieth-century office equipment. I know we cannot hold rebellious groups that want to go charismatic and pull all the cash they can into their pockets, but our ABI here is putting some good men out into the work. The other group covets these people for their side. Of course we do not want to see splits, but it gets to the point where we simply have to hold the line, let the rest go, and pray that one day they will return in a different mood."

Around this time, unemployment in Brazil had peaked at 44 percent. Some of the church folk simply had no money and would not have been able to get by were it not for the land on which they could grow their food. Not only that, the mission had been hit by severe and unexpected financial outlays. They had tried to import a Minolta copier that cost over $5,000 in the US and more than $10,000 in Brazil. The local distributor somehow found out about the copier coming from the States and bought off customs officials to stop them. They lost $7,000 in all but finally did receive the copier. Then Bennie had to buy two new engines in one term for the 206. Termites and rot had so weakened the floating hangar that it had to be rebuilt. Compounding the problem, some utility bills had gone up 600 percent. The DeMerchants, however, had long learned frugality and adjusted to the difficult situation.

In spite of problems, Bennie preached three services in a row, each in a brand-new church that they, as missionaries, did not help the congregation build. Two of the churches had a capacity of over two hundred. The DeMerchants believed strongly in piling responsibility on the shoulders of loyal, trained men—sometimes almost more than they could handle—but were glad to see the men pitch in and do their own sacrificing, working, and giving.

To add to their reason for "forgetting those things which are behind, and reaching forth unto those things which are before," the DeMerchants worked with their missions director to establish the Faith Promise plan and Partners in Missions. As a result they were able to appoint two new families for Mato Grosso and Santa Catarina, two states in Brazil with a population of several million people that were without a UPCB church.

Bennie added a personal project to his over-busy schedule. He wanted to recognize the ministers in Manaus in appreciation for all their hard work. He invited all of them, four or five at a time, to go out for a late-afternoon break to camp out in hammocks and fish a little the next day before returning to the city. The place he had in mind was only about twelve minutes away in the 206 and in cellular range at night so he could keep in touch with Theresa.

In this way, Bennie felt he could get closer to the ministers, especially the younger ones coming into the work who had good churches started. The relaxed atmosphere of the jaunt would provide him an opportunity to hear some of their problems as well. A few of the men would take a light and a prong, and spear a few fish while the "finny folk" were sleeping alongside the waters near the shore.

Because of his job as overseer of the work in Brazil, Bennie often flew commercial airlines when visiting churches in and around the larger cities. One time, however, he flew into a new area of Brazil's backyard. He landed the Cessna 172 on a reservoir at Cascavel, Paraná, where the Brazilian government had built a dam, creating a reservoir behind it. The site, twenty-five hundred feet above sea level, is not very big. Since no floatplane had ever set down on that pocket of water inside the city limits, the landing was a real novelty to the locals. Even the television personnel appeared and covered the arrival of the plane for the nightly news.

On October 29, 1996, the DeMerchants celebrated thirty-one years of being in Manaus. Their labor in Manaus alone had resulted in sixteen churches. They had divided the city into ten sections and the Amazon State itself into seven districts. When representatives from each district sat on the National Board, some ministers from the South did not like the Board being overweighted toward the North. Bennie suggested to the representatives from the South that they work harder and grow more to balance out the representation.

Traveling seemed to broaden the vision of his board members. A 45-hour trip Bennie made in the 172 to Paraná State south of São Paulo with his missions director changed the man's perspective tremendously. Everywhere they stopped and with whomever they talked, the man found open doors and gracious reception in enormous states with modern life, huge farms and ranches, and mechanized farming. They splashed down in almost thirty places coming and going and took their time, preaching with their brethren in southern Brazil.

In Londrina, Paraná, the church folks met them at the river nearby and, after securing the plane, drove them to a packed church pastored by an elderly couple who had helped many start churches, with the younger men testing their ministerial wings in the South. Lourivaldo and Caroline Polycarpo had the two stay in their apartment above the church. (Lourivaldo ministered in that church till he was in his nineties and later went on to his reward.)

Always a strong supporter of Bennie, when any criticism arose over an issue Lourivaldo would stand up and ask the assembly, "What has this man done for Brazil but good? You all need someone in our faith who is not ashamed to stand up and tell us where we are going and what we believe. We need to hold up his hands and follow him!"

Brother Polycarpo's name was highly respected among all of the southern brethren, who in the lack of resident foreign missionaries could be influenced to lean toward liberalism. He convinced many to hold the line and follow Apostolic doctrine and did not hesitate to sound the alarm—even into his nineties. Polycarpo and the other ministers he influenced held the church on track so they would not tend to loosen up on such standards as mixed bathing and watching television. When Bennie saw so many able-bodied ministers with their wives willingly retire in their sixties just to have a successor and be the senior pastor or pastor emeritus, he always thought of Brother Polycarpo, a non-quitter with a strong, positive voice.

Bennie Jonas DeMerchant, a son on loan from God for sixteen years

They sorrow not as those who have no hope.
Theresa over her only son's grave in New
Brunswick.

At the same time in this life God has given them
many sons and daughters in the gospel in a faraway
land!

José Ribamar de Lima

Most Brazilians do not have an easy, carefree life. One fourteen-year-old boy, José Ribamar de Lima, slashed the tall jute plants with his sharp machete on Marecão Island in 1969. All family members and neighbors worked hard in the knee-deep water to harvest this cash crop. The river was quickly flooding the lowland flats where this fibrous plant grew, and soon the water would be too deep for harvest. While whacking away with his machete, José did not notice an anaconda snake that had washed downriver overnight and was twined into the edge of a small pile of jute bushes. As he turned around in ankle-to-knee-deep water, the snake lunged from behind the boy, its weight almost knocking him down. José screamed for his dad nearby, who rushed to help the teen kill the crushing water serpent.

Due to the Amazon's constant floods in lowlands, his family moved ten miles downriver to Manacapuru to look for better farming conditions. They found higher ground northwest of town where they could get away from the annual floods and grow better-paying crops than jute.

Manacapuru, only fifty miles west of Manaus, could be reached by bus or car. The DeMerchants with a few others held street meetings in front of the town's main market.

Theresa would pump her accordion while they all sang, testified, and passed out tracts. Sometimes they would spend the night in the cheap hotel nearby. From this small group that gathered around came other contacts who were interested, and the DeMerchants followed their invitations, including one to Marrecão Island. This land had very little value in that it flooded, so arriving from way upriver, the people who settled there got it practically for nothing. But as life improved, they wanted out after seeing river floods. Sometimes in the night they would open their door to see water flowing east all around. At times they would disturb an anaconda that had washed down against the wooden set of steps or poles their house sat on in the water.

In 1969, Christian workers sent from Manaus preached the gospel on an island in simple house meetings near the growing town. José and his dad were among the first who attended these meetings. They found salvation in these meetings and turned their lives over to God. After finishing high school in this city, José desired to attend Bible school in Rio. The DeMerchants had observed Brother Lima's zeal for hard work, so with assistance from the Ladies Ministries, they sent him on the twenty-eight-hundred-mile trip by boat and bus to Rio de Janeiro to attend Bible school operated by missionaries Robert and Jean Norris.

In 1979 after graduating from ABI in Rio, Brother Lima returned to Manacapuru where he accepted the pastorate of a thatch-roofed church with three families. Under his leadership the church quickly expanded. Later, after his humble church was set on fire and burned to the ground, he received funds from the late Beatrice DeMerchant's memorial and built a large central church.

Eventually the work in this city expanded to fifteen churches. From that state capital west of Manaus, over one hundred more churches sprang up through his leadership abilities. Brother Lima acquired a commercial fishing boat, which he licensed and with hired hands made a few runs hundreds of miles up Amazon River tributaries. They would catch up to twelve tons of freshwater fish and store them in a huge box of ice. Then they would return and sell the fish in the Manaus markets and help finance his many outreach church projects.

Trained workers were badly needed to go hundreds of miles farther west on the Amazon or its tributaries to secure many of these works. After Manaus, Manacapuru was the first city to start and operate a two-year Bible school. In 1994, Brother Lima started the second Bible school in Northern Brazil in the balcony of his central church in Manacapuru. From there, using boats as the only means of travel, trained young couples evangelized new towns and started other Bible schools in key areas. Funds were usually limited with the nationals, but they were willing to work on projects if there was food on location! Often a group of ladies accompanied these projects and prepared food for all the workers who were sawing hardwood directly from tree trunks.

Teams of carpenters and bricklayers went to help build more new churches. They dropped trees with power saws, stretched chalk lines, and sawed lumber on location or used portable cement block forms to make blocks for many new churches on the Solimões (Amazon), Japura, Purús, Madeira, Negro, Juruá and Tarauacá rivers. The natives always knew the type of wood to cut that did not quickly rot or allow termites to destroy it. Any funds sent by the DeMerchants' American friends and relatives usually went to purchase aluminum roofing sheets. If that material was unavailable, Amazonians would cut down a palm tree, open its fronds branch by branch, and form it into a thatched roof. The only drawback was that these roofs could be easily set on fire by some enemy of the church when no church people were around! Fortunately, this rarely happened because the troublemakers themselves lived in that kind of dwelling.

The DeMerchants' seaplane brought missionaries and workers to visit key areas for conventions, seminars, and special occasions. Soon this huge new area had over a hundred churches and had to be subdivided four times into river districts for administration. With the help of textbooks from the Ladies Ministries, each one of these new districts started other Bible schools of 620 hours of classroom time in two years.

One time, Brother Lima and six other men had to use a power-saw brigade to slash and hack their way through twelve miles of swamp bringing mechanics, mineral water, food, canvas, hammocks, and tools to Bennie, who was stranded in the middle of the jungle. A cylinder of the engine had blown off the 206, forcing him to radio for help and execute an emergency landing in the rainforest.

Another time Brother Lima was with Bennie in Cruzeiro do Sul, Acre State, a city right next to Peru at the head of the Juruá River. After having a church meeting the night before, and sleeping in a small wooden hotel, the two men crossed the river in a canoe taxi to an eddy where the plane had been safely sheltered from the floating debris of the swelling river. When they grabbed the wing strut of the seaplane and got ready to untie it, armed federal policemen stepped out of the jungle and took them to their paddy wagon on the city side of river.

After arriving at the police office, the two men were interrogated in separate rooms, the police asking Bennie and José the same questions: Why are you flying a plane in this area? Where did you refuel last? Why are the backseats out of the airplane? Where did you spend the night? What did you do last night? Why did you store the plane on the other side of the river from the city?

Bennie and José, although in different rooms, gave the same answers. The policemen worked hard to get a conviction, working through the night to get evidence, checking out the registries of the expensive hotels in town. They checked every nook and crack in the airplane where aircraft maps and charts were stored. They looked in the back pockets behind every seat. They screwed open every gasoline jerrican and sniffed the contents, looking for the smell of ether, something used in processing drugs.

Later Bennie learned that the federal agents went to the business establishment where Bennie bought regular gasoline in jerricans and questioned the cashier. He was asked if he noted Bennie's wallet when he pulled it out to pay—was it fat or skinny? Did he see any large denomination bills? Were there any hundred-dollar American bills?

Apparently the officials thought they had nailed a drug-running airplane. To their thinking, an owner of an airplane that can land at millions of natural airports on Amazon water systems way out in the boonies had to be on a drug-running operation. All they needed to do was to close in on those involved and realize a big reward. After meticulously questioning the two men, the police released them to fly back to Manaus and Manacapuru.

Perhaps the government agents were remembering a tragedy that had occurred several years earlier. Peruvian drug patrols shot down a floatplane owned by a Baptist mission that took off from Benjamin Constante near the Peruvian and Colombian borders on a flight plan to Iquitos with three Americans aboard. The flight plan had not been communicated to Peruvian air traffic control, and the craft was intercepted by the Peruvian Air Force, flying an American-furnished plane with high tech weaponry. With all that fancy equipment, and trigger-happy, they started shooting at the mission seaplane, killing one of the missionaries and her baby that was in her arms. The Peruvians kept shooting, their bullets breaking the pilot's legs. The pilot was able to land on the river, but the Peruvians continued to shoot at it in overhead passes till it sank in the river. The damaged seaplane was recovered, and close to twenty-two bullet holes had pierced the floats. A barge brought them to Mission Aviation Fellowship seaplane hangar in Manaus. Bennie had sent aviation fuel in barrels to that Baptist mission for many years to have fuel on hold for mission work in the area.

In 2006 Manacapuru reached a new landmark. The UPC of Brazil, under Brother Lima's leadership, built Jerusalem II, a general meeting place for churches in their district. A round-roofed structure a mile to the northwest of the central church, the Jerusalem II Conference Center occupies a small block with a seating capacity of three thousand. It has both a low platform and a high one with a cement slab for instruments and choirs. The Manacapuru ABI then moved into air-conditioned classrooms there that can accommodate 120 students.

Then in 2010 they went to a jungle area where a paved road connects Manacapuru with Novo Airão on the Rio Negro, and ten miles out of town built a huge metal-roofed, brick-sided "prayer shed" that can be reached by road or by boat. Sometimes three thousand young people at a time from the twenty-five churches in the Manacapuru area go there in boats or buses for all-night prayer meetings. Till midnight those kinds of services are just worshipful singing and preaching. Maybe at 3:00 AM they stop and have a snack and then continue on until daybreak.

In 2003 when the UPC of Brazil reorganized, the country was divided into four national regions with twenty-nine districts and about one thousand churches. Pastor José Lima was elected northern regional supervisor of the UPC of Brazil, Amazon Region. Among his other duties, he visits seventeen UPC districts and 650 churches in his area of the Amazon Basin. Look how far that fourteen-year-old boy has come!

Cutting jute, a back-breaking job

Thank the Lord for . . . Malaria?

A very fine family named Melo lives in Cruzeiro do Sul. Antonio and Simão (Simon) Melo graduated from a Baptist Bible school. After that, they went to college and married college-educated women who also became captured by the Word of God and involved themselves wholeheartedly in the work. The two husband-and-wife teams of the Melo family are college level teachers and know how to organize a Bible school, run churches, and inspire people for missions. With great zeal the family cooperates and coordinates their efforts to start new works in villages and small towns along the tributaries and into the Amazon Highlands near the border with Peru. Simon is the district superintendent for west Acre; Antonio moved to Rio Branco and pastors a missions-minded church on the east side of that state. The work there is booming and Antonio's wife, Luciene, heads the ABI there. Being a college-trained pedagogue, she is well qualified for her position.

In Simon's large church Bennie saw something he had never seen before in any church. "Simon must have forty or more people who come in on motorcycles, a common conveyance for these farm folks. Shelves on the back wall near the coat room provide smoothly sanded and varnished cubbyholes for their motorcycle helmets," Bennie noted.

In Cruzeiro do Sul, the pastor and staff thoroughly educate their young people and instill in them a spirit of missions. At these headwaters of the Juruá River, many creeks and side roads provide access to the land where the rural people plant manioc and raise cattle and poultry. In fifty-four small villages and towns of two hundred to five hundred people in the Amazon Highlands near the border with Peru, the youth go into these villages, borrow a lot, and pitch a tent. They take their instruments and soundboxes, and sing, preach, teach, or anything else that needs to be done to get works started. People come out of curiosity to see what's going on. If nothing happens in a place after three months, the youth just pull up their tent stakes and move to another area.

Sometimes these young people pile into their own cars to make the 145-mile run to Tarauacá to fellowship with the work there. This help and strength from the larger church proved literally to be a lifeline to the smaller churches in that area of Acre a few years ago. A demonized man thought like a witch doctor and followed every idea, vision, dream, or daydream he got from the devil. He convinced a few of his followers that he needed their help to kill some people in a tiny, remote village. They rampaged through the small cluster of dwellings and clubbed or sliced into oblivion six or seven people, including an old man, a child, and some teenagers.

The rest of the villagers fled and reported the massacre to the nearest police station miles away downriver in Tarauacá. An investigation probed into the murders. The place was so remote that it took the police several days to reach the site of the mayhem, a small clearing at the head of the Taurá River near the Peruvian border.

When the police finally nabbed this fellow, they took him to Tarauacá, the nearest town with a police system and local court. The demonized man told the police he was a pastor of the UPC of Brazil, and the police copied that on their report. This man might have visited a church once, maybe even watched a church service, but he was never a member of any of our churches, nor was he a Bible student, worker, or minister of any category of our UPCB fellowship. After questioning the man, the judge ruled him a mental case and put him in a local jail.

The nearest newspaper publishing office was in the state capital of Rio Branco, Acre, where Antonio Melo pastors a thriving church. Brother Melo had baptized a few people of another denomination and, as usual, that made their pastor mad. Someone from this same denomination worked at the newspaper office, saw the police report, and leaked it to the newspaper reporters.

The newspaper jumped on the story and had a field day using negative publicity about the UPC of Brazil for weeks, always finding more erroneous things to report. These reports spread through newspapers, television, and even in national magazines. They drew ugly designs that filled a full newspaper page or a double-page spread in the middle, portraying the UPC as a wild bull with long, widely extended horns. They also published a picture of a huge snake coiled up, its mouth open and fangs curled with the UPC of Brazil placed beside the bull or the snake. Some authors of paperback books concocted gruesome stories with the cover depicting rape of a young girl, with a title about religion going to the extreme. The murders were terrible, but to deliberately connect them to the UPCB as a denomination and to continue promoting such a false report was not only wrong but also grossly defamatory.

Without bothering to verify the story, the national papers and television picked up on this and ran with it for days until Bennie had to get a lawyer to insist the press prove the truth of their stories. It did not matter to them that this was an untrue report that had gone to international news media—even Reuters reported it. It was a false accusation against the UPCB, but it spread all over Brazil.

The bad publicity caused such a backlash that some of the members of the congregations in the South were afraid to attend their churches. Bennie knew what the false accusers were doing in the newspaper, radio, and on television, but he just had to slog through it. When the case reached the courts, he was never called to testify even though he was the president of the UPC of Brazil!

Some workers had been trying to start a church in Tarauacá. The saints in nearby Rio Branco and the infant church at Tarauacá cringed at the way the media had blown this incident and reported error after error. The UPC of Brazil reiterated that this illiterate man never was a member, never was a worker, never took any ministerial course to be a worker, and never was a pastor. His name was never printed in their annual publication listing ministers by name, category, addresses, and phone numbers, but the media refused to accept the organization's attempts to set things straight.

Bennie was so furious he wanted to jump into his 172 seaplane and fly down to this town and walk into the authorities' offices to reason with them. Instead he ended up in bed with the worst case of malaria he had ever had. All the time he was sick he prayed about the situation. As sick as he was, a spirit of laughter engulfed him when he thought about what the devil was trying to throw at the church. Bennie felt that Satan sensed a great harvest of souls was coming to that area with the preaching of the Word. Even through his sickness, Bennie felt the hand of God and believed the whole problem would end up glorifying God and bringing victory.

Months after the murderer was put in a prison for the insane, Bennie flew over to Tarauacá. When asked by the airport who owned the aircraft, Bennie stated on the microphone "the United Pentecostal Church of Brazil" and gave his pilot code. He could tell they were taken aback.

He splashed down in the Tarauacá River to a hearty welcome by folks in the church. They were delighted that Bennie had finally come in the church plane. He mentioned the murders when he preached in the church meeting. He reassured the saints there that the demon-possessed, mentally deranged man had no connection whatsoever with any of the UPCs of Brazil. Furthermore, he explained that the opposition to the message used the report as an opportunity to put down the UPCB churches in any way they could. His upbeat, reassuring report greatly boosted the church's morale.

The church in Tarauacá not only survived, but today it has a Bible school. Of all the sixteen districts in the Amazon, it has become the most fruitful not only with large churches in seven surrounding cities, but also with numerous rural places and Indian tribes in between. Workers trained in ABIs in Eirunepé, Envira, Carauari, Ipixuna, and Cruzeiro do Sul use five large 40-foot aluminum canoes and one boat to service the area.

Each of the two larger churches in Envira has a radio program alternating every day. The miracle of a pastor in Envira having had AIDs before coming into the church weighing only eighty-five pounds before being baptized and receiving the Holy Ghost testified to the healing power of God. This pastor now works with business people in that town, which also has three smaller churches. He uses one of the 40-foot aluminum canoes and other church boats in Cruzeiro do Sul, Eirunepé, and Ipixuna with energized workers who will run even in rain, day or night, to reach people. In addition, five ABIs are training the youth who come into the churches and deeply desire to let the Lord use them.

At the UPCI General Conference in 2013, Global Missions presented a challenge to raise $5,000 for helping start a new church in each country. Bennie's regional director, Darry Crossley, asked Bennie where a likely place would be in Brazil. Bennie placed Feijó, Acre, on the list.

Feijó is a neat, clean farming city twenty miles east of Tarauacá on the head of the Feijó River, a tributary of the Tarauacá River, which eventually runs into the Juruá River near Eirunepé. In highwater season, powerful tugboats push barges up the crooked rivers through the jungle in forty-five to sixty days and nights with food and hardware supplies for the towns of Tarauacá and Feijó. Then Brazil's federal government asphalted the final 450 miles of jungle mud road and built bridges to connect Tarauacá with Cruzeiro do Sul at one end and Rio Branco at the other. After the Acre District helped purchase a lot by payment plan, Global Missions sent half of those funds, and the building in Feijó houses a fine group of worshipers.

Now, in 2015, the whole Juruá River drainage is in revival and is a model district for the rest of the UPC of Brazil. With thousands of miles of well-built paved highway from Cruzeiro do Sul to Rio Branco, and then on to Porto Velho, Cuiaba, São Paulo, Rio, and other huge southern state capitals as far south as Curitiba, Florianopolis, and Porto Alegre, they enjoy a transportation system that not even Manaus with all its industry, tourism, free zone trade, petroleum, and other economic benefits in the Amazonas capital can compete with. So all those who heard and saw such derogatory condemnation of the UPC of Brazil are now seeing firsthand the effects of training men and women for the work. Only God knows how far all this will go.

All the ministers in Acre are excited about the rapid growth of the work and the great future they have. The full double-middle page designs, television reporting, radio, and even Reuters who thought they were defaming the UPCB in front of millions of people have only contributed to the present explosion of His name being preached everywhere.

The people in Tarauacá told Bennie later that if he had gone up there with his plane, the people would have set the plane on fire and stoned him because of what they were reading in the false reports of the newspapers and hearing on the radio. The only way God could keep Bennie out of Tarauacá at that difficult time when he was so upset and wanted to fly down there was to lay him low with malaria.

Sometimes God has an unusual way of working!

All dressed up and ready for church!

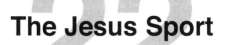

The Jesus Sport

The DeMerchants feel theirs is a rich life. They have been tested to the limit and blessed beyond abundance. Although they have just about had to go "hermit" with their families and put the work above all, they realize Jesus said it had to be that way. Bennie notes they have been at the same location longer than Moses lived in the wilderness. After their nest emptied, Theresa's exceptional skills led to her total involvement in training Bible school students.

In the middle of it all, Bennie has been able to relax and practice the Jesus sport. Jesus never kicked soccer balls, hit a home run, or played golf. But He often took His disciples away fishing. It is the quietest sport. Just to duck out for a few hours with his fishing rod renews Bennie. Popping away to the nearby jungle lets him escape from faxes, the ringing doorbell, people coming and going at the house as if it were a bus terminal, folks needing assistance, wanting used clothes, asking to make phone calls or send e-mails, helping coworker missionaries, addressing the national church and district problems, foreign missions department requests and communicating with supporters . . . he often works past tiredness.

Even if he is unable to wet a line, he appreciates being where he can drop into a hammock and sleep early after a tropical 6:00 PM sunset. After a nap that renews him, he may awaken in a low hammock, and half sit up and pray for everything he can think of. He might walk around in the moonlight, or sit in the plane tied up on the bank and pray, meditate, or write up sermon starters in his Day Timer.

Those things, along with a good dose of humor (especially in laughing at himself) refresh him. To think on the things the Lord has brought about in the work beyond their earliest, greatest dreams revitalizes him. But Jesus did take the disciples away fishing, filled the congregation more than once full of fish before ministering, showed the disciples how to fish, baked fish on the beach before calling them to eat, and told them where to fish when the IRS got after them.

Brazil offers thousands of places, watery and otherwise, in which to practice the Jesus sport, whether the fishing spot hides in a huge city, perches on a silt-built island, is tucked into a small village edging a neighboring country, or lurks along the thousands of miles of riverbanks.

Manaus is an island of urbanity in the middle of Brazil's rainforest with boat or plane the only links to the outside world. It is an enclosed world living inside this isolated jungle capital. The focus of local newspapers seems short-sighted. Headlines of the local newspaper blare in large bold letters the scores of local soccer games of sports clubs or of a fatal fight between prostitutes with gruesome, enlarged photos of the murdered person on the front page. News of the outside world would usually not be covered or, if found, would be inserted inside the paper in a short, brief column. Such news is considered too irrelevant to the interest of the average soul surrounded by this immense jungle. It is a treat to pick up a days-old newspaper from the outside world that an airline passenger has left at the airport.

Marrecão is a real island in the middle of the Amazon. It measures nine miles long and is shaped like a half-moon, and floods during the highwater rainy season. Located just above the turn of the Amazon at Manacapuru, it was created from silt from the floods and changes slightly every year end. The people on this island farm it by hand. With jute as their cash crop, they harvest corn, manioc, sugar cane, and vegetables. They perch their humble houses on stilts at least four feet above the ground. Before the rainy season catches them, they transfer their livestock to higher land among relatives near Manacapuru. In rainy season the river swirls around and beneath each home.

These folk visit the open markets well stocked with farm products, small hardware, materials for making clothing, and so forth. After they purchase their supplies, they hang their hammocks in relatives' homes to visit and sleep overnight. The next day a friend with a canoe helps paddle through the eddies and backwaters to return them upriver. Sometimes they catch a passenger boat that leaves them near their home for a small fee.

Decades ago, Pastor Manuel received some of these folks as visitors in the humble church service in Manacapuru. The friendly, hospitable people invited him to visit their island homes and have church in a larger dwelling. Almost all these very humble and hard-working people seemed to be interrelated. It was the setup for a revival.

To the DeMerchants, this island of silt that changed annually and contributed more silt to the city below and built up another huge island there from nothing symbolized the move of God throughout the Amazon. His Spirit moved like a river and transformed people and their lives wherever it was allowed to take them. While the DeMerchants worked in the city with its complications and many attractions to establish His church in urban areas, the islander Amazonian people in rural areas grew stronger and stronger. The DeMerchants would labor in the city and from it train the ones who reached into the rural areas, villages, and towns and evangelize both at the same time, constantly fishing for men.

Many of these Islanders had family in Eirunepé and begged the DeMerchants to go and tell their families there the wonderful Acts 2:38 message. In the early 1970s, soon after Bennie had flown the Cessna 172 to Brazil from the US, he had started to plan the 750-mile fishing trip to that faraway western town. After sending aviation fuel on ahead by barge and storing it in trustworthy villages along the way, he visited Eirunepé. Eventually a thriving church was established and became the hub for the whole region.

Years later, on a circuit flight to preach at Eirunepé and other churches in this region, Bennie flew over a small town called Bom Futuro (Good Future) on the Jutaí River. It was about the last stretch of water long enough to land and take off. His fuel was running low; he needed a place to touch down so he could refuel the plane. This sparsely populated area maybe averaged one dwelling in twenty miles, so when he spotted a house with a canoe tied up in front on the river, he knew people would be somewhere around even though no one was in sight.

Stopping at a dwelling where people live brings one to some sort of civilization in case the engine won't start or the battery grows weak or other problems develop. People in these places rarely see an airplane. They may marvel when the strange bird lands and people emerge. Even a small plane is bigger than it looks in the air. By the time Bennie lands in places like this, he has often seen the whole family disappear into the jungle.

After climbing up their riverbank, he will shout, "I am Pastor Bennie from Manaus. All is well!" Sometimes an old man will come out into the edge of a small field, holding a shotgun. Bennie tries to look harmless and shows that he is unarmed. The two men close the distance between them, and after the usual Portuguese greeting and stating his purpose, Bennie watches the old man signal with his arm and from the jungle his wife and kids emerge.

Near Bom Futuro, a young woman was living there with her parents. When Bennie first saw her she had a tiny child in her arms. They told Bennie a story that nearly broke his heart. The younger woman also had a little six-year-old boy. Three or four days earlier in the late afternoon the child had skipped down to the river to take a bath. When the youngster did not return to the house, they began looking for him.

Mother and grandparents hunted everywhere. When they could not find the child, they suspected an alligator had caught him. The rural jungle man usually keeps a box of shotgun shells in the house. The older man filled his gun. He went out and started shooting the closest gators nearby, killing several. One of the dead gators had shreds of the boy's shirt between its teeth. They slit the reptile open and found the pitiable remains of the little boy.

Shaken by the horror of the story, Bennie talked with the family an hour or two. Before he left, he handed them a stack of used clothing and some literature. He also gave them five liters of precious auto gasoline because at the head of these abandoned rivers none is available. The gasoline was a big gift because it would save these people hours of paddling upriver against the current when they returned home after going downriver to town for supplies. The largest city close to them with a UPCB was Jutai, 450 crooked miles downstream. Eirunepé was 140 miles south using a crow's wings, upriver and over the watershed to a jungle trail that eventually widened into a jeep track and then a makeshift road into town.

In practicing the Jesus sport, one casts a net wherever one can. The net may come back empty, but then again . . .

Pamela with her catch

Keeping the BLD Airlines Airborne

Just keeping the vital planes in flying order requires a bushel of work. The Cessna 172 has had ten engines since 1968; the larger 206 has had six engines since 1975. Maintaining the various components, the VHF radio systems, having the transponder for radar checked out of plane by an approved shop every twenty-four months, and keeping the insurance and legal work with ANAC (the FAA equivalent in Brazil) up to date keeps a person scrambling.

Then the pilot has to be certified in three areas. Every year he must undergo an exhaustive physical that includes even his driving and behavior records from the police and a psychologist's evaluation. Every two years he must suffer the tricky written pilot exam on ever-changing air regulations. The final test happens every twenty-four months when an inspector climbs into the copilot's seat and checks out Bennie's flying skills. Bennie counts this as the easiest part of the certification process, even when he does certain types of in-air maneuvers within tight restrictions.

Some people have asked Bennie, "Will your airplane land anywhere?"

Bennie says yes. "It will land anywhere, even on a tree or a building or in the town dump. The only thing is that afterward it will not take off."

God makes the difference. Once as Bennie boarded an airliner, the captain saw the seaplane pilot's association sticker on his handbag.

"Do you fly?" the captain asked.

"Yes," Bennie replied.

"What kind of planes do you fly?" the curious captain asked.

"Single engine seaplanes," Bennie answered.

"How many hours do you have?"

Bennie responded, "Thirteen thousand hours."

An astonished pilot exclaimed. "And you are still alive?"

"Well, yes," Bennie said, "but I have a lot of stories to tell since I soloed at age eighteen in 1959, have been medically fit since, and am still current."

By the mid-1990s, the Brazilian government had obtained their own floatplanes and developed airstrips for wheeled planes, so Bennie's services to the government were no longer needed. The downturn to this resulted in there being no more barrels of leftover aviation fuel to help support the mission. The upshot meant that Bennie was well known at many Indian outposts and during the years had developed a remarkable familiarity to the topographical aspects of the whole Amazon Basin.

Both DeMerchants love the Bennie Leigh DeMerchant Aeronautical Company. "All one has to do is pay attention on landing and taking off," Bennie says. "The rest is simply to hold the nose straight on the invisible road you point it on and it will get you there. No drunk drivers careen around up there and most of the birds dive as you approach them. Of course one has to fly through an occasional thunderstorm on instruments, but maintaining heading, altitude, and speed will bring you through the rain and out into the sun. Even if fifteen minutes seems like an eternity, you can put your sunglasses back on later. God bless and pass me another can of aviation fuel. It only costs $10-$12 a gallon around here."

For Theresa, it means she doesn't have to take off her shoes and pull the pins from her hair to pass through security. She can carry anything she wants—even a kitchen knife if she is so disposed! No long concourses to traverse, no escalators to ascend or descend, no crushing crowds of people, no narrow aisles to squeeze along. Instead, after she arrives at the edge of the river with the seaplane backed in tail-first, she takes only four or five paces from the double-cabin pickup truck to the flat tops of the plane's pontoon. She steps up on an aluminum foot-like ladder and turns around to sit on the pilot's seat. A pull from V bar behind the windshield scoots her onto the copilot's side. What a pleasure it is to have BLD's Airlines spoil her with her own loving pilot and private plane!

Recently Bennie has discovered the joys of training a new young pilot. The trainee helps fuel up the seaplane that when empty holds eighty-four gallons of fuel. First he must siphon that out of fifty-five gallon drums into jerricans of nine gallons each. Step two, he has to carry the heavy jugs from their church depository down over a riverbank. Step three, he must climb up on the floats and swing each jug up onto each wing before pouring the gas slowly into a fine mesh-screened funnel.

The sweat pours also when the outside air temperature registers over one hundred degrees in the shade. Fueling up in the heat of the day is not a job Bennie likes when the chore can be done near sunset or early in the morning. However, if someone else offers to do that while the elder Bennie swings gently in his hammock taking his afternoon siesta to charge up his own energy battery for evening service, Bennie will not object!

Such refueling had occurred when Bennie and his trainee took off last year in the 206 from Coari on the Solimões River aiming for Pauini on the Purús, a 385-mile one-way flight. An hour into the trip, Bennie noticed the fuel gauge sinking from full to three-quarters full quite early. With fuel tanks full the gauge float in the tank usually stays longer reading full, then drops fast from three-quarters to one-quarter, and slowly bottoms out from the last quarter to empty.

"Did you fill the tanks while I was taking my siesta yesterday?" he asked his new helper.

"Yes, I did," the young man replied.

"Both sides?"

"Yes."

"Was the seaplane floating when you did this or was the front pulled up on the shore?" Bennie persisted in his questioning.

"No, the front of the floats was pulled up on the shore."

"Hmm. Did you know that seaplane tanks use a different procedure from wheel planes?" Bennie asked. "A wheel plane on level asphalt has to be filled up at the outer wing filler to remove the big air bubble that remains. A seaplane must be floating. With your weight and fuel jugs on the float of the plane on that side, the wing tip will drop and completely fill to the inner filler gas cap and run out the top. That must be repeated on the other wing to get the full fuel range of the aircraft. Otherwise you could be short thirteen gallons of fuel."

Oops! That explained the low reading on the gauge.

No problem. They'd be able to reach Pauini and buy fuel from other air taxis.

When Bennie checked the fuel at Pauini, he was somewhat concerned. It seemed they could return to Coari to their fuel stop, but due to the refueling error, they would have a very low reserve. The good news was that the last hour of the flight would be over the Coari River and lake that empties into the Solimões at Coari. Without at least an hour of fuel, Bennie would never think of leaving the water, a "natural airport" always underneath and within gliding range, to cut across the open jungle.

So the following day Bennie and his trainee took off and flew at the plane's lowest economy power settings. Several times, Bennie prayed they would not run out of gas. If they did, it would take a full day for the local people living along the river to make the run into Coari to get his own aviation fuel stored behind the church and return. Bennie and his trainee would have to wait with the seaplane tied up at the shore in front of the hired helpers' dwelling.

With low fuel in the left tank, they raised the wing a slight angle to the horizon so all the fuel in the wing would run into the drains to the fuel system. They flew until the engine sputtered. They quickly switched to the right tank with auxiliary fuel pump engaged, and the engine roared back to life. Next they raised the right wing to a shallow angle and flew with the ball left of center on the turn and bank instrument. Flying thus, all the fuel available would be drawn out of the right tank.

Bennie looked down several times as they soared over the Coari lake and noticed that the water was very calm and the surface looked like a mirror. Thank God for no headwinds! Twenty minutes before Coari came into view, he observed that even with the tilt of the right wing, the fuel indicator was reading below empty. At any moment, he expected the engine to quit. He scanned the shore, searching for scattered huts with a canoe tied in front, an indication that the inhabitants were at home.

Before they reached Coari, Bennie spotted a big thumb of land bulging into the lake. They dared not cut the distance shorter by a straight line from where they were and leave the "airport" below, so they followed the bulge all the way around but stayed well within gliding range from the water. At any second, Bennie expected the starved-for-fuel engine to quit. After they rounded the bulge of land, they sighted the city and turned straight in, holding altitude till finally they were within gliding range to the water in front of Coari. After they splashed down, Bennie expected the engine to quit idling. He grabbed the paddle to finalize the trip. They pulled the mixture to lean and the propeller wound down to a stop and they coasted forty feet toward the shore. Bennie's helper pilot slipped from the plane, grabbed the rope, and tethered the front rope cleat of the seaplane's floats to a small tree on the shore.

Out of curiosity, Bennie went to the drain cup to release any fuel left in the system. When he pulled the fuel drain under the aircraft's engine injectors, not one drop formed to plop down into the cup, which normally will hold half a glass. Nothing. They had flown on fumes.

After they refueled—properly this time—they headed for Manaus. In fifteen minutes they ran into a rainfront with such high winds that the GPS showed a drop of 50 mph in ground speed and this held almost all the way to the hangar on Lake Aleixo. They looked down on the wide Solimões River where white caps curled on the water and barges headed for the nearest breakwater along the shore. When they landed in Manaus, the gas tanks registered an hour and a half of reserve fuel. They had learned to take precautions so God could free the angel that protected them for a greater mission for someone else.

Farther Out: Across the Atlantic

Bennie loves maps of every size, coverage, and scale. When he first went to Brazil, the maps of the Amazon River Basin contained wide blank spaces. Now, fifty years later, the maps are far more accurate, and at times roads lace the land below the wings of the floatplane.

Sometimes students from the rural areas knew little beyond the river's two curves above and two curves below their homes. To expand the students' minds and help them understand about distances, Bennie made six large maps on huge sheets of Styrofoam for missions classes. He started with a map of greater Manaus and their bus routes that took over an hour for them to come to class. Then they progressed to a larger scale map of the Zona Franca, the bigger area around Manaus. As the idea of paper representing distance started to develop in them, Bennie moved on to show them Manaus County; then the Amazon State. He expanded his map to include Northern Brazil, and then all of Brazil. Another of his maps showed Brazil's place in South America. And finally he showed them a map of the world.

"Manaus is the fastest growing per capita city of Brazil, increased by 86 percent in exports in 2006," Bennie taught them. "There are oodles of jobs and over two million in

201

population, but this city is just a pinhead on larger world charts."

Bennie also taught them some principles of GPS operation. Students loved it—it opened their eyes to their responsibility to others and to think and pray more than ever for missions. Deeply integrated into this teaching was I Timothy 5:8, "But if any provide not for his own, and specially for those of his own house, he hath denied the faith, and is worse than an infidel." The DeMerchants taught that although this refers to natural substance, it includes providing the gospel to the whole "house" of Portuguese-speaking nations, especially since no other Oneness group was seriously doing so. Thus, in the 1980s and 1990s, the Bible schools in Brazil taught missions classes the need to carry the Jesus Name message to other Portuguese countries, which have a combined population of well over fifty million people.

Brazil itself has a population of two hundred million and is the only South American nation with broad industry. The country stretches almost as long north-south as it does east-west, and despite the watery expanse of the Amazon Basin covering approximately 50 percent of the land, can boast to being third in road mileage in the world, second in total airports, and third in aircraft production. In spite of being predominantly Roman Catholic, Brazil has more "evangelicos" and offers greater religious freedom than the USA and Canada.

During the World Conference in Malaysia in 2000, Jim Crumpacker and Jerry Richardson approached Bennie about Brazil's sending someone to help establish the UPC in Mozambique, a war-torn country bordering Malawi. Fugitives from Mozambique had fled to Malawi and some visited one of the churches in Malawi and got saved. When they returned to their own country, they asked for help.

Bennie, as head of the Brazilian church, accepted the challenge, but the idea of the UPCB sending missionaries abroad needed repeated promotion from north to south and east to west throughout all Brazil for the people to catch the idea of supporting their own "foreign" missionaries. They would need costly airplane tickets, an apartment containing basic electro-domestic appliances, and literature in Portuguese. A vehicle and funds to travel to visit the local church groups were a must. They would give seminars, hand out books to ministers, and do the work of an evangelist. A vital to-do on their list was to start Bible schools to train the church members who desired to advance His kingdom in their country.

The UPCB selected Cesar and Vilma Moraes and their two teenage children for the opportunity to grow and stabilize a Jesus Name church in Mozambique. An experienced and trained third generation Oneness Pentecostal Brazilian, Brother Moraes claims that God spoke to him in the classroom that he would be a missionary to one of the other Portuguese-speaking nations.

Before the end of 2000, Bennie and Cesar flew across the Atlantic to the southeast coast of Africa to visit Mozambique as tourists to give Cesar a first-hand impression of what he and his family would face.

After Brother Moraes returned to Brazil, the Moraes family traveled the Basin and other larger UPCB church districts to raise partners for their mission. After gaining the necessary support, the family left for Africa in 2002.

The Brazilian people are a can-do bunch. They took on the project of building an ABI in Portuguese Africa and Central Mozambique to train men to reach that nation and others similarly cultured. The Brazilian UPC missions program has faithfully and liberally supported this family since then. The Ladies Ministries of Brazil furnished the Moraes's apartment with kitchen and office appliances, furniture, and beds. For seminars, thirty boxes of Portuguese literature were sent to help train Mozambican church leaders. Six years later after districts were formed and after seminars, church meetings, and conventions were held, Mozambique had become better organized. The Brazilian church brought the Moraes family back to Brazil in January 2007 for their deputation.

Brother Moraes's annual field report sent to Brazil in late 2014 included the following points: In Mozambique he and his wife load their car with literature and hold seminars of thirty hours each for the scattered ministry of the UPCM in SóFala, Tete, Manica, and other provinces. They work with the native people to purchase basic foods for meals at these and other locations. They move constantly and visit many local churches over weekends.

The central church, pastored by Brother Moraes, includes a walled-in area large enough to grow vegetables. They have erected walls for a Bible school and seminar location for the country. Much is left to be done, but they are well located in Gondola, a city several hours of travel north from Maputo, Mozambique's capital. The property is on the main paved east-to-west highway in the center of the country that connects the city of Beira on the Indian Ocean to the western African countries on the Atlantic Ocean.

While in Mozambique, the Moraes's son Wagner grew up and married a Mozambican lady who worked as an airline attendant and got in the church. They worked with his parents for a term in Gondola, and then relocated to Maputo. Brother Wagner and his wife Theresa currently hold meetings in their rented apartment; they use a motorcycle for transportation. Undaunted, they purchased land, walled it in, and raised up walls for a church building. As soon as funds come in, they'll put the roof on.

Brazil has many irons in the fire for missions and presently all "matching funds" have been depleted from the grand idea of jump-starting works through Regional Missions—Brazil broke the system! Under the Regional Missionary program championed by Brother Howell, a relatively recent initiative by the Global Missions Division, countries in which the UPCI has missionaries can now send missionaries from their own converts to other, unreached countries. As a result, by 2015, forty "extra missionaries" have been sent by these evangelized countries.

William and Bonnie Markham served as missionaries in the state of Goiás, Brazil, for ten years. In 1990, they were transferred to Lisbon, Portugal, where he now oversees the work in both Portugal and Spain. A highly valued saint in Portugal, Alcina Lima, retired from the Brazilian government. A lawyer, she poured herself into the work there by writing and translating volumes of material for Portuguese countries and books for the Bible schools. This wonderful lady also translated *Full Throttle* into Portuguese. She died in 2013.

Roni Querino, his wife, Ana Paula, and their two children from Rio Grande, Brazil, work in Porto, in the northern part of Portugal. They have a fine rented flat above a business place in a prominent part of the city. He worked in real estate and pastored in Brazil, so he knew how to get a church set up there. They already have about forty constituents in a growing work.

Guinea-Bissau is a small, Portuguese-speaking country located on the northwest Atlantic coast of Africa. They gave resident visas for Brazilians to start a church there. In 2014, Sileno and Nadia Souza accompanied Edino Zonta and Bennie to Fortaleza, Brazil, via Cabo Verde Islands, Dakar, and Senegal, intending to arrive four days later in Bissau, capital of Guinea-Bissau. The Souzas had obtained a one-year visa from the Guinea-Bissau embassy in Brasilia. In spite of all their careful preparations, the trip soon developed nightmarish, exceedingly expensive qualities.

To begin with, Cabo Verde Airlines delayed departure twenty-four hours and put them all in a hotel. When they arrived at their first stop in Praia, Cabo Verde (Green Cape), their changed tickets required extra fees to allow them to board another airline whose baggage allowance was very low. The four travelers had parceled out 240 Portuguese Bibles and other cell ministry materials into their baggage; they got charged again on that. When that second airline also was delayed, they could not connect in Dakar with the ongoing flight that had been missed, so once again the group had to stay overnight at a local hotel.

Since they would be leaving the airport for the hotel, the four of them had to purchase visas. Everyone at the hotel spoke French. Bennie, being the only English-speaking person of their party, hunted all over to find someone who could speak even a smattering of English. Then the taxi driver gave them such a literal run around in heavy, bottle-necked traffic at night through alleys, back roads, and rough streets, they wondered where he was going. A second taxi, loaded to groaning axles with baggage and literature, trundled along, adding to the mounting expense.

When the foursome returned to the airport the next morning, they learned their pre-purchased flight tickets were not on the proper day and were useless. Once again, Bennie hunted for an airline clerk who could speak English, only to discover that the one available flight was full. They paid for their tickets in American money, and eventually it was decided they could board the next flight. They received no tickets, but just stood around until they were called from the counter. With Ebola running amok in the surrounding countries, sometimes their passports were checked in six locations between getting inside the airport and onto the plane.

It took a week for Bennie and Edino to find the Souzas an apartment with a large room for having services and to leave them somewhat settled in. The Souzas now have meetings with up to forty people in one of the famous new countries of the world where the UPCI has helped the Brazilian church reach across the ocean. The church group is looking at lots on which to build a central church in Bissau.

Guinea-Bissau is the only country in the area that, as of this writing, has not been hit with Ebola, but people are afraid. "We could read the tension from airport personnel wearing medical gowns as they eyed every passenger," Bennie noticed. "If one of us were to be pulled off with some visible defect and put in a quarantine station, it is difficult to know when and how we would ever get out of there. I feared that even more when Edino and I got back to Brazil and saw reports in the papers of the problems with Ebola in countries surrounding Guinea-Bissau.

"In spite of it all, I was amazed that everywhere we went we heard people speaking Portuguese and understood them just like in Manaus. I am sure the country will become a strong Oneness church base from which we can move down the coast."

Angola is the third Portuguese-speaking country on the African continent. "We have been asked about trying to help open up Angola, southwest Africa, a Portuguese nation of twenty-two million people with a high cost of living," Bennie declares. "The economy centers largely on mining gold and precious stones. Already we have seasoned and trained men and women pastoring churches here in Brazil who want to answer this call."

A few years ago, Angola was under communist control,

having received troops from Cuba while various factions fought to dominate the country. This changed later, but anti-evangelical roots still remain in the system. No visa even for a tourist is given by their embassies abroad without a connection to a person, place, and reason that person would be coming to Angola. One ray of hope when working with the Angola government is that a visa for a month is available for people who are residents or citizens of other African countries.

Brother Edino is trying to get two more Portuguese countries opened by sending a couple to the Cape Verde Islands, a group of nine islands in the Atlantic Ocean off the coast of northwest Africa, about six hundred thousand people, and also into Portuguese Principe e Tomé, another duo island country farther down the African coast. A third group of islands, the Madeiras, dot the Atlantic north of the Canary Islands and lie due west of Lisbon, Portugal. The work there is supervised by Bill Markham.

One really can be amazed by how much God is interested that the gospel be heard in all nations by His church on earth. After arriving in East Timor, an island nation about five hundred miles northwest of Darwin, Australia, on March 7, 2004, with Mark Hattabaugh, a North American pastor who was raised a missionary and grew up in Argentina, Bennie and he were both surprised to see the Portuguese language on signs in the country. They were twelve time zones ahead of where they lived in Manaus and Miami. After flying three days by jet to go around the world, their internal "clock" was out of order with it being midnight in East Timor while it was midday in Manaus, so they took a taxi to a modest hotel in Dili to get some rest.

While en route to the hotel in the taxi, Bennie spied a sign on another street that had the word "Pentecostal" displayed on it; he quickly marked it in his GPS. At the hotel, they checked in and fell into their beds, sleeping till late Sunday afternoon. When they rose, they caught a taxi to take them to that Pentecostal church. It was pouring rain so hard that the windshield wipers, overcome with the force of the deluge, provided only the barest visibility. As the GPS dropped down to the point Bennie had marked, the rain stopped at the iron gate of the church. Brother Hattabaugh and Bennie got out and clapped their hands, the customary thing to do rather than bang knuckles on steel.

A woman wearing a long, white cape answered their summons, and they presented themselves as Pentecostal pastors.

"Please, come in," she invited them. "My husband is the pastor of the church. He is praying with an elder in the church right now."

The woman hurriedly prepared a snack while Bennie and Brother Hattabaugh sat at the table in their parsonage and began to talk with her. Before long her husband, who introduced himself as Brother Bernardo, joined them.

Then he startled them by his next remark. "While we prayed, the Lord showed us that two men were looking for me," he revealed.

Talk about encouragement! To their delight and amazement, Brother Bernardo invited them to speak in the Sunday evening service quickly coming up.

After an exciting worshipful evening service, Brother Bernardo suggested they drive with him the next day to visit and preach for five nights at some of the preaching points where he had six hundred people spread out in the mountains. Bennie thought that was a great opportunity and an open door.

However, when he and Brother Hattabaugh arrived at their hotel, he received a message that seemed to slam that door shut. His mission headquarters of the UPCI in

Missouri, USA, requested that they wait two days to meet a delegation from the UPC of Indonesia and Australia at the central Post Office at 2:00 PM on Tuesday, and if the delegation did not arrive, to return on Wednesday. That seemed to ruin their plan to visit and preach at other places with Brother Bernardo.

Before daylight the next morning Bennie rolled out of bed and onto the floor, praying flat on the carpet. It seemed they had flown around the world to one of the oldest Portuguese-cultured countries that had been torn by war, and now felt it was a wild goose chase without the opportunity to minister to more people.

"Lord, if it is Your real plan that we try to reach all these other Portuguese cultured countries as here, please do something extraordinary today so that I will know we are in Your perfect will," Bennie prayed one of his God-busting prayers.

Wow! What a prayer! Bennie got up, dressed, and the two men walked to the front of the hotel to a coffee shop where they sat down at a table to make their breakfast request to the waiter. They had hardly seated themselves when two men pushed through the door and sat down at the next table. One of them had a small emblem of the flag of Brazil on his shoulder.

Bennie decided to have some fun with him. So in Portuguese, Bennie asked him what he was doing so far from the country that sings like this—and he sang the first line of Brazil's national anthem to him. The man came unplugged with surprise at an American guy singing perfectly in Portuguese. They began a ping-pong series of question and answers.

Bennie asked, "Are you from Brazil?"

"Yes!"

"What part?"

"The Amazon."

"What city?"

"Manaus."

Then it was Bennie's turn to get unplugged.

"What suburb of Manaus?"

"Cachoeirinha."

"What street of Cachoeirinha?"

"Ramos Ferreira."

"What number on Ramos Ferreira street?"

Then the man asked a question. "Why do you want to know so much? I live at number 55."

Bennie reached over with the biggest smile he'd worn for a while and exclaimed, "I live on Ramos Ferreira Street in Manaus, Brazil, and here we are twelve time zones away around the world on a planet with seven billion people!"

Bennie could hardly believe his eyes and ears, because when God wants to do something extraordinary it can blow a person's mind! That experience taught him that what one person can casually brush off as a coincidence or luck, there is no lottery better than God's numbers. Such an encounter will never happen again in his lifetime. That experience underscored his firm belief that *God is wholly interested in missions and that He wants the whole gospel preached to the whole world by the whole church!*

Shortly thereafter while in the same region, Bennie went alone to Macaú, off the Chinese mainland near Hong Kong. English vessels sailed to Hong Kong and traded with the Chinese a century ago while the Portuguese claimed Macaú. The place is small; he could walk around the gambling and prostitution dens and still find common people in 2004. Bennie delivered on foot all kinds of Portuguese literature kits to all Christian churches he could find using the Yellow Pages at the hotel. Today, in 2015, Macaú is being reached by the church in Hong Kong.

"Just a few days ago I saw a picture in one of our publications of a person in Macaú being baptized in Jesus' name by one of their workers," Bennie reports with great delight.

Encouraging news comes from another Portuguese-speaking country that lies north of Australia in the Indonesian Archipelago. Amidst heavy persecution, Brother and Sister Bernardo Guterres, leaders of the independent Pentecostal church of Timor Leste, have been baptized in Jesus' name. This has opened a door in that country for the furtherance of Oneness Pentecost.

How thoroughly do the Brazilian churches support missions? Take, for example, the church in Coroado, a suburb of Manaus, which Edino Zonta pastors. The district superintendent of the largest UPC district in Brazil, East Manaus with over 160 ministers, he is always promoting missions. Zonta's church is aiming to give to missions a hundred thousand reales this year—and another church has challenged his and is trying to surpass his church in giving. Offerings from those two churches combined would be over $50,000 US!

Brazil is reaching farther and farther out, crossing ocean waves and circling the globe for the Lord!

Farther In: Up the Rio Negro

A strong spirit of missions has overtaken the Brazilian church with the desire to reach farther and farther in along all the tributaries and streams of the mighty Amazon to every tribe of Indians in northern Brazil. This delights and amazes the DeMerchants, because most Brazilians look upon the Amazon as a place of poverty, Indians, no industry, and poor education. In their zeal to see His kingdom grow, the DeMerchants prayed prayers far beyond their imagination, prayers they thought to bust God, but He played their hand. They did not pray to become millionaires but for Jesus and His name to be known and His power to fall and change lives.

The Brazilian government does not want outsiders interacting with the Indian tribes inside of their reservations. Interlopers have exploited the Indians in order to line their own pockets with profits from lumber, cattle, mining, and even drug trafficking. However, from the late 1970s to the early 1990s at the behest of FUNAI, Bennie had flown hundreds of medical or mercy flights into these tribes. The Indians had learned he was their friend. During the same time span, the government was educating the tribes by teaching their children Portuguese, and translators were putting the Bible into tribal languages.

To add to teachers and medical personnel going into the tribes, the Indians themselves started coming out to the large towns and villages to trade for items they needed. As these people from the heads of the rivers came in contact with civilization, they began trading Brazil nuts, cassava meal, and other commodities for money to buy fuel for their propeller-driven canoes—rather than paddling against the current in the high temperatures— and became dependent on trade from the outside.

Although Bennie and his workers were forbidden to evangelize these tribes, eventually some of the Indians brushed shoulders with saints who had a passion for witnessing. Over time, the Indians began to invite Bennie and his workers to their villages, and the government had to respect these invitations made by the Indians.

"The government cannot forever prohibit the outside world from moving in among these people when they tire of paddling and want motors for their canoes," Bennie says. "Then they have to go to civilization to buy parts and gasoline and oil. On occasions when they reach the cities near the mouth of the rivers they live on, they also come in contact with our people and pastors. Our pastors are advised to treat them well for the gospel's sake and follow up every invitation they get to take the gospel to them."

Then they visit a UPCB church . . . well, guess the rest.

Most of the land reserved for the Indians lies in the Amazon Basin, the DeMerchants' front and back yard. The first Indian group to be reached was the Satere-Maue tribe at Maral, the FUNAI outpost near Maués in the year 2000. The Satere-Maue people make a very popular fizzy, cola-type drink from the guaraná plant. They roast the seeds, grind them to powder and mix the powder with water. The men drink this liquid before going on a hunt because its high caffeine content quells hunger while giving them plenty of energy. The drink is even commercially available on the Internet!

Two groups of the Moura tribe, one in Borba and the other near Autazes, were reached in 2004, and both groups now have church buildings. In the same year, the UPCB was able to touch the Ticunas near Lago Grande of Santo Antonio, near the mouth of the Içá River that empties into the upper Solimões. This populous tribe is an anomaly: its language is an isolate, meaning that no other tribe speaks it and it is not related to the general basic language, Tupi Guarani, an Indian language spoken throughout South America.

In helping the Indians with education and health matters, FUNAI's task is made much easier if they bring them to one location, build an airstrip, and ferry teachers and health personnel in and out, rotating them every thirty days or so. FUNAI encouraged these near Santo Antonio on Lago Grande to move closer to an outpost with shelves stocked with modern basic medicines that a doctor or other trained medical personnel could have quick access to.

"We have a huge following of several hundred Indians near Santo Antonio do Içá on the upper Solimões River where beyond this city, on Lago Grande, we have built a church," Bennie reports. "Local pastors in the area help them. The trick is to present something without foreign influence. Top notch Indians from Rio Negro received a grant to study for a degree at a college, only to wind up graduating from ABI with high marks and returning to their own people with the message. The missionary program and studies develop a heavy burden in their hearts to reach their fellow Indians, no matter what tribe. Voilá! A church is born. Besides that, these Indians have easy access to other tribes."

The teachers and doctors intermingle with the Indians in a friendly way and sometimes they even sit in on church services with UPCB ministers. Churches are easy to start but resident ministers need to be located nearby till the group becomes mature. Bible schools must have a trained teacher in the vicinity with books and an interpreter. In just about all the tribes and villages, a tribal member who has been exposed to modern civilization awhile—maybe for extended health treatment of a family member—meets a church member, who in simplicity and acts of love or donation of items, touches and reaches the tribe.

The year 2004 also saw the church going against the current by reaching north on the Rio Negro to Terra Preta and the Ingatú, who not only had a church but also a Bible school. By the year 2005, the UPCB was working with over one thousand Indians in various tribes close to Manaus.

The Rio Negro district was formed in 2009. Among seven tribes of Indians, twenty-eight of their leaders have graduated from ABI and are eager to reach all the tribes in the areas where Bennie and his troops cannot go. The new district superintendent in Novo Airão is a strong leader with a large church in Mao with thirty-five alumni that he has constantly working on boats reaching new areas. A nurse from the church in Manaus, Maria Gorete, who with her nursing aid Nazaré, would teach the Indians from a large boat they anchored nearby. They would also travel by canoe to Indian villages and go ashore to have church and teach lessons to the tribe.

The seventy miles of road from Manacapuru to Novo Airão was paved through the jungle and the town has become a tourist center with presentations with freshwater porpoises. The Indians are in a reserve on the opposite side of the river, which one has to cross through the Anivialianas, an archipelago similar to the Thousand

Island area of the St. Lawrence River in Canada. They are reached by boat from Manaus.

In one Indian village, Marau Novo or one close to it, in ten days, 120 received the Holy Ghost and now they were eager to reach every other tribe in Brazil. By 2011, Bennie wrote that "they were presently working in the seven tribes of Indians that soon will be nine, two with whom we have been asked to move in with a pastor and start a Bible school."

Further up the Rio Negro, the town of São Gabriel da Cachoeira sits in the center of a vast area that is home to four tribes: the Yanomani, Baniwa, Baré, and Tucano peoples. Since Indians form a majority of the town's population, it is quite possible for one church to reach several tribes in this area. The UPCB achieved this in 2010.

Bennie reports they had started a work with the Yanomani out of Boa Vista at the eastern edge of the region. However, some Trinitarian folk were able to persuade the Indian chief to block the work. Bennie feels that all of this is going to come to nothing and the work will rise up quickly when the right people come in and the truth hits them.

Bennie has flown dozens of times to the Iauaretê Indian outpost of FUNAI almost on the Colombian border with Brazil, with the northern Brazil FUNAI director, dentists and doctors, carrying Styrofoam boxes with vaccines on ice. This village lies near the equator above São Gabriel da Cachoeira. On April 15, 2015, the DeMerchants were delighted to receive the following invitation: "Pastor Bennie, you are invited to dedicate a UPC of Brazil in the rural area of São Gabriel da Cachoeira on 23 of May in the Indian tribes of Baré and Ticuna."

Aviation fuel for such trips can be critical. Even regular gasoline is unavailable in the season when supply boats cannot get over the shoals of this low water, rock-filled river. Once Bennie left fuel reserves with a friend below the city, but the military confiscated them without advising Bennie of any infraction he'd committed, so he has learned to anticipate anything when trying to work in the area. The whim of the investigating officer can be the law of the land.

"The officials cannot believe that one is operating a private aircraft in the area with any motivation other than drug trafficking or flying in equipment for drug labs in the jungle," Bennie says. When in a pinch, his most powerful response is to meekly give a soft answer: "This airplane only needs a three-hundred-foot stretch of water to take off into the wind. With millions of places in the huge Amazon system with this minimum operational area, would I come and land in this city knowing there are police and fiscal agents here and be caught doing something illegal?"

At Pedras, on the Içá River on the Brazilian side of the Colombian border, Bennie had a good wait before the seaplane could be liberated for takeoff until radio contact with Brazil's central security system could be established and his name entered into their computers. He needed clearance from the head offices in Brasilia.

Bennie says, "It is a satisfaction to know that no intercepting aircraft in Brazil can shoot you down without a final clearance from the National Federal Capital Ministry of Aeronautics in Brazil. Finally the truth hits them: It is just ole Bennie, Benir, or Benice, as they may call me, running around to his churches in his Pentecostal mission seaplane!"

The Tucano Indians occupy the region near Tabatinga where the Javari River pours into the Rio Solimões (Amazon) from the Peruvian Andes mountains. This interesting tribe is a multilingual people because men must marry outside their language group: a man who marries a wife who speaks his language would be viewed as committing a kind of incest! Men choose the women they marry from various neighboring tribes who speak other languages. Language learning seems to interest these people and most of them can speak most of the languages. This polyglot is accepted as normal, and speakers move readily from one language to another in the course of a single conversation. In fact, the Tucano shift so easily from one language to another that they are hardly aware of doing it!

Enthusiastic missions workers have made inroads up the Rio Negro into these Indian tribes positioned mainly along the river and its tributaries, but like kids with their hands in the cookie jar, the workers plead for "just one more."

Bennie with Canamari Indians on the Xeruá River

Edino Zonta, UPCB director of missions

Nadia Matias and Sileno Guerreiro, regional
missionaries to Cabo Verde

Bread upon the Waters

Scattered along the Mapueira River, about eighteen villages of the Wai-Wai Indians sustain themselves by hunting, fishing, and planting manioc and other vegetables. Bateria, a remote Wai-Wai village of about seventy-five Indians, sits almost on the equator between two sets of rough, churning rapids as the river pours down from the Guyana border.

Lying farther downstream, the village of Mapueira is the Wai-Wai tribal headquarters. Health and educational centers manned by the government provide the twelve hundred Indians there with a high level of education in Portuguese. An airport for wheeled planes allows teachers to be rotated every four to six weeks with others from Santarem or Oriximiná. Both a large rectangular roofed church and a round communal thatch-covered structure will hold fifteen hundred people.

Southwest of the Mapueira River, the Nhamundá River separates the states of Amazonas and Pará. It also runs southeast, roughly parallel to the Mapueira. At some points in the hilly jungle, the two rivers are only thirty miles apart. Indians can walk across this stretch in three days or so. The Nhamundá eventually flows past the city of Nhamundá to join the Amazon River.

The Hiscarianos live mostly on the Nhamundá River with their main headquarters at Cassawá, also called Nhamundá, with about nine hundred people. The Brazilian government maintains health and educational personnel there also. After tumbling over nineteen sets of rapids below Cassawá, the river borders several villages with a population of one hundred or fewer in each one. Villagers walk between the rivers for festive occasions and often intermarry with the villagers on the Mapueira River.

A third river, the Jatapú, southwest of the Nhamandá, generally parallels it. Many Hiscariano Indians have migrated to the Jatapú. One village, Santa Maria, perches below the first rapids, which are difficult to pass in dry season and become turbulent, frothy white water in the rainy season.

All of these rivers have many sets of roiling rapids, although as the rivers approach the Amazon the land flattens out. At the mouth of each of these three rivers, cities have sprung up: Nhamundá, São Sebastião, Urucará, and Oriximiná. The Indians come to these towns to buy such foods as rice, beans, and sugar; household supplies such as knives, hammocks, kerosene for wick lamps, tools, and hardware; and fuel for their small gasoline engines, which they use to grind manioc and to propel boats or long dugout canoes. The UPCB has churches in these cities, and the pastors and church leaders have been instructed to do anything possible to help the Indians whom they may meet when the Indians visit their city.

The Indians along these rivers have an innate distrust of outsiders. A group of interdenominational folks have worked with these natives since the early sixties and consider them as their own project. This organization looks upon the UPCB as invaders, and has done its best to stop the Jesus Name message from penetrating their areas. They consider those who preach the new birth as recorded in the early church in the Book of Acts as "non-traditional Protestants." They worked for decades to translate the Bible into the Indian dialect—and were frustrated to see Bennie and his trained workers swoop in and successfully teach the Indians the great doctrines of Oneness and Jesus Name baptism.

A few years ago, Bennie was flying in that direction one day and out of loneliness, decided to throttle back and splash down in front of their city of round, thatch-roofed houses in Mapueira just to see who and what was going on. The people were glad to see him. Then a few days later the Wai-Wai village leaders arrived at the DeMerchant home in Manaus and invited them to open a mission.

"We could not reach them till we had their invitation to do so," Bennie explains. "These Indians were abandoned by the Trinitarian group about seven years ago. An older man who saw me working with FUNAI years ago told us that he prayed every day for some time that we would come back, but we had no one to place there."

So in 2011, the UPCB raised an offering of $8,000 for Indian Nations missions. The church tapped Marcelo and Marciane Braga as UPC of Brazil tribal missionaries to work among the Wai-Wai. At this central headquarters of Mapueira, the Bragas lived in another home while Brother Braga, with help from the local Indians, built a comfortable, large mission house. With financial aid from the national missions and Bennie's budget, Bennie airlifted a refrigerator-freezer, a lighting plant, a stove, a bed, a mattress, outboard motors, and even an aluminum canoe tied backward on top of one pontoon. (He filled the left wing with fuel to offset the weight and balance problem!)

The UPCB found fertile ground for the Jesus Name message in that region. Using the canoe, Brother Braga traveled the river visiting the villages he could reach within a day's travel. Paul Reynolds, from British Columbia,

Canada, helped the UPCB finance the church construction in Bateria where Brother Braga has baptized about fifty or more Indians. The village chief built a one-room house for a place for Bennie to relax and spend the night. It provides enough space for a couple of hammocks and a plastic table and chairs. Bennie showed his appreciation by giving the chief precious gasoline for their use.

The Bragas spent over a year working with the Wai-Wais in Mapueira before injuries and other health issues forced their returned to Manaus. However, during part of that year, the opposition flew in some of their men to teach the Wai-Wai Indians at Mapueira that Bennie and the UPCB missionaries were false and not to follow them. The Indians mostly obeyed them, but Bennie jumped over Mapueira. Soaring over rocks and rapids, he put his workers upriver above them at the remote, difficult to reach Wai-Wai village of Bateria. The UPCB folks were able to work there and baptize about forty-five people and pray with them. One thing Bennie knew was that the Trinitarians, even though they got on the radio and denounced Bennie and the other workers, were unable to quickly and easily move into this area by boat where no airport for wheeled planes exists.

"When we get enough of the Wai-Wais in Mapueira on our side by baptisms, they will one day revolt," Bennie believes. "That may not be far away. What brought the headquarters group with their airstrip and medical and educational facilities on location toward us was their knowing we were flying things they needed and desired right over them and on to Bateria above a rock pile they could not easily get over in dry season. The two-way radio system throughout all the villages broadcasts news of the things we flew in and gave them. That 'casting your bread on the waters' will work after many days and it is what we need to get the message to them so they will listen. It is worth the sacrifice."

Not long into 2015, Bennie told the chiefs at a meeting with them that "we hope to get your tribe here in the true message so we can support you to reach every tribe in the rest of Brazil." That was a limited prophecy statement, but the Indians were maybe flattered that someone would have that much faith in them.

The UPCB also helped the Hiscarianos build a church in Santa Maria, cutting hardwood beams out of the jungle with power saws. The structure, which will hold about 250 people, has concrete floors, brick sides, and school desks for children. It could also serve as a Bible school. Bennie has a 28-foot aluminum boat there that the builders used for hauling materials from the jungle for the church construction. Nasário Mera, an ABI graduate, licensed minister, and handyman without peer, led a crew that cut termite- and rot-proof hardwood from the jungle nearby. It was a very hot, sweaty job, breathing the exhaust of power saws in the sweltering, suffocating heat and humidity of the day.

The head of this village, Manoel, who was baptized in early 2013, wants an ABI started among his group at Santa Maria so his sons and other relatives can be more knowledgeable about the Bible. However, finding the personnel who will stay there and conduct the Bible school is the big problem. Bible-school-trained people from rural settings seem to serve better than those uprooted from the city with all the modern conveniences. To meet the logistical needs, it looks like the planes of the BLD Airlines will come in handy for a long time!

Other than flying, the UPCB has a second way of reaching Santa Maria. The church has a long, 40-foot aluminum canoe with high sides that can carry up to three people and tons of supplies. Before his health forced him to leave the area, Marcelo and one or two men accompanied him to Santa Maria in a long, hard, two-day run with a 15-horsepower outboard motor. This ministry team has baptized about forty people there.

Going between the Hiscariano villages of Santa Maria and Cassawá by water would be like going from New York City to Boston via Chicago, so Brother Nasário wanted to cut a shortcut through the jungle. Part of this jungle trail would follow an old open iron mine road extending about thirteen miles northeast/southwest and only about thirty degrees off the compass to the true route, but at least it would help shorten the jungle trek by ten miles. If a trail could be established between the Hiscarianos at Santa Maria and the other families of their tribe at Cassawá, the Indians could hike rather than follow the long, crooked river route that included pulling the canoes over nineteen sets of rapids. From the plane, Bennie and Nasário calculated that in three to five days it could be walked and marked on the ground using the GPS.

A plan was established: a man would go upriver by boat to a meeting point at a creek entry on the Nhamundá River at the approximate time estimated for Nasário and his crew's arrival. Using Bennie's GPS and plenty of batteries, Nasário and six Indian men hacked a trail thirty-three miles from Jatapú River to Cassawá. The route was far more mountainous under the green jungle canopy than it looked from the air. Nasário and his team had to back up at times to avoid some cliffs and to find springs of water in the jungle valleys. At night they made small fires and took turns standing sentinel while the others slept in hammocks strung between two trees. A bit of interest was added to their adventure early one morning as they trudged downhill in the jungle: they encountered a large jaguar just ahead, padding uphill toward them. Dairo, Nasário's brother-in-law, grabbed a shotgun and pulled the trigger.

All he heard was a click. The humidity had affected their hand-loaded cartridges. With the jaguar creeping toward them, all Dairo knew was to yell "Jesus!" and pull the trigger again. The second time, the shotgun boomed and the big cat turned and fled the other way.

Then their food supply ran out.

Fortunately, Bennie had included a big bag of peanuts in the food supply and told Nasário that on a rainy day or when food ran low, the peanuts would give him some energy. The trailblazers finally got to the river after nine days, but the fellow who was to meet them with the boat on the fourth or fifth day waited until the eighth day and then returned to Cassawá.

Arriving at the Nhamundá River at sunset, the men tied floater logs together with green vines and pushed their makeshift raft out into the current. They hit some rocks and had to retie the raft a few times, but at last they staggered into the outpost worn, tired, and hungry. They rested a couple of days and decided that the shortcut between the two rivers was not a feasible plan for travel. The low-risk boat trip took less time than the jungle trek!

Bennie flew them all back to the Jatapú and then Manaus in the 206 in just a few minutes.

All outposts with fifty or more people have two-way radios and chit-chat a lot. When Bennie flies over one of these places to go to the end of the line, like the remote area around Bateria, they report from four places Bennie flies over that "Bennie went by . . . at such and such a time," so when Bennie gets to the village, the people have congregated there on the riverbank to wait for him. It seems that the sound of the seaplane's engine hardly fades out from one village till another hears it in the distance. As it goes overhead, they automatically report Bennie's position. Of course, whatever is brought in also is reported, like clothes, foodstuff, and fuel. "We cannot feed and clothe the whole Amazon," Bennie says, "but for those of our household of faith in extremely remote locations and without economical means to acquire such items, we have assumed a responsibility."

So although the Trinitarians did all they could to block the UPCB out of the headquarters of Wai-Wais in Mapueira where the Bragas lived and worked a year, on the next river south, a bright spot emerged among the Hiscarianos. Santa Maria has converts who are following the mission of the UPCB, and some in other villages who know the truth are planning to switch rivers and move to Santa Maria. The village is located halfway between Manaus and Bateria, so Bennie skips the plane over watersheds and can be in Santa Maria in about an hour and a half.

The Hiscarianos at Santa Maria and the Wai-Wais in Bateria and Mapueira village headquarters have begged the DeMerchants, "Please send in a pastor and start a Bible school." Some of the chiefs have told Marcelo that when they go to Manaus they want to be secretly baptized in Jesus' name. No one tells them what to do when they get off the reserve, and they want to follow the Bible examples of the Book of Acts. Edino Zonta already has baptized one chief along with his wife and daughter in Aleixo Lake, right beside Bennie's floating hangar.

"We have three leaders there also who follow us and we take them all kinds of things that they can use," Bennie reports. "We would like to see these people filled with the Holy Ghost, but in a service and alone it is hard to get them to leave the idea collected in their mind by other church groups that when one prays, one carefully chooses the right vocabulary while all the others listen and no one shouts or gets excited. But this will all change in time and if we can manage to bring them into our conventions in Manaus and in the atmosphere of several thousand people praying, all things will happen."

They all like the things we bring but are fearful to invite us at times, even to speak in the church at Bateria that we helped them build. But the truth cannot be stopped forever. If we train some in Santa Maria, they will pull people who speak their language in with them. The six Hiscarianos who attended our meetings at the Jerusalem Convention Center in 2014 loved it even though most of them did not understand Portuguese.

Sometimes our people shy away from being close to the Indians from the jungle because the Indians are always asking for something— they have very little or no money. So when we visit these river towns, we fill the airplane with practical things we can take to them and this helps in a way to hold them as much as possible with us. We leave behind such things as clean used clothing and rolls of tough fishing line, including boxes of 9-aught fishing hooks and sinkers. They whirl these around their heads like helicopter blades and throw them a long way into the pools below the rapids where fish are lurking.

During Easter weekend, 2015, Jonathan DeVall and Bennie airlifted a full load of goodies in the 206 and delivered half to the ones in the church at the Jatapú River falls and half in Bateria.

Bennie also feels encouraged by things that happened during Easter at the Mapueira river Wai-Wai headquarters:

The main opponent to our working there had to leave for Oriximiná to have health treatment for his wife. After an Easter festival in their

229

huge communal round house with about 800 in attendance, Brother Edino Zonta had them distribute 50 pounds of pre-packaged candy to many outstretched hands. Afterward we were privileged to have a two-hour question and answer session as to why we were not working with them even though we built a mission house among them and sent Marcelo and Marciane Braga to live there and work with an aluminum canoe and motors to evangelize the villages up and down the river. We just advised them that we felt blocked and heard that our names were maligned over the party line radio each village has. We advised these twenty or so leaders that Trinitarian missionaries preached about 90 percent of what is in the Bible but left out the other 10 percent which contains the most important salvation issues.

Bennie further added that even Jesus did not go where He was not invited! "If you want us to leave, just say the word," Bennie said, giving them the choice and acting like he was under their command. All went silent and then big smiles broke the solemnity of their faces.

"They all wanted us to come back," Bennie continued. "If we roll our marbles right it will be easy to see the five thousand people of the Wai-Wai tribe, after decades of work with linguistics folks who put the Bible into their own language in their hands, to come to His name."

Working with Indian tribes in evangelism can be slow work. No one can be brought to Christ without first making friends and gaining their confidence. It starts with recurring friendly contacts at the bottom of the scale till one gets to ABI graduates on the top. The main objective is to get the gospel out to all possible people and at same time stay subject to the laws of the country. If the UPCB is advised that they are not to go into some of these areas with a boat or airplane, they have to pray and obey. On the other hand, when Indians come out of their area, the contact and transfer of knowledge is inevitable. This has also happened in the west with those on the Biá River near Carauari who walk over to this city on the Juruá River. Pastor Janio at Pauini advised Bennie of meetings they are having with another tribe, the Guajaha.

In early 2015, Bennie preached the dedication service of a new church on the Xeruá River for the Canamari Indians near Itamarati, a town halfway between Carauari and Eirunepé. Delcio Carioca, a hard worker and school teacher, at times trudges six hours through the jungle carrying heavy loads from a Juruá River loop overland to the Xeruá. Carioca not only pastors a church in Itamarati, but will walk overland with many of his church people to the Indian church to minister to over a hundred of these Canamari Indians where a church has been built at Flexhal village.

While away in Urucará with Edino Zonta at a ministers meeting of Lower Amazon District ministers, Bennie got word from a woman member that they are working on the Andirá River with their Pastor Alfonso in Barreirhna, a city with modern facilities and an airport behind a long island about twenty-five miles southwest of Parintins.

"She told me that we have a church in Andirá River that has oodles of Indian villages going up it to the south," Bennie continues. "That was a surprise! She reported that we also have a church among the Sateres Indians in a village on this river at Boas Novas. Also surprising is that we have a lot of new places in Amazon River villages east of Manaus now that used to be a strong area of the Trinitarians."

Oh, Lord, bring on more surprises like that!

UPC among Indians of
Xeruá River, Amazonas,
Brazil

Marcelo and Marciana
Braga, missionaries to
Indians in 2014

Bateria village on the
Mapueira River, near the
equator

Return to the Abonari Outpost

In the early 1970s, with all the activities going on in the area and no one else with aircraft capable to land on water in the small, narrow headwaters, for a while it seemed to Bennie that he lived behind a whirling propeller. At times he spent nights at the river bridge camp on the Alalaú when he did not finish his flying jobs early enough to return to Manaus. Bennie got to know where the Indian huts were on the huge Atroari-Waimiri reservation like the back of his hand, using only the shape of jungle hills and distant jagged peaks on the horizon for orientation.

The little Cessna 172 would put-putt-putt low over the Indian huts. Swooping over these clearings with naked Indians running around below, Gilberto Figueredo would toss out loose bags about 50 percent full (to avoid breaking on impact) of rice, sugar, manioc meal, flour, beans, salt, and dried pork for beans. They had delivered mirrors, fishing hooks, line, machetes, files, axe heads, medical supplies, soap in bars and in powder, and updated newspapers from the outside world to the Indians, road workers, military personnel, and FUNAI bridge crews to the outpost for over twenty years until the government was able to land wheeled planes and helicopters on the road.

The Atroaris and Waimiris were the wildest groups. They occupy the extreme north of the state of Amazonas, south of Roraima, in the area of the Alalaù, Camanaù, and Curiuaù rivers. These Indians for almost a century had acquired a bad reputation for white man's incursions— probably over a hundred men had died from their arrows. The jungle highway from Manaus north to Boa Vista was completed around 1975, but not before it had brought devastation to the tribes through a long series of deadly epidemics that reduced their population to around three hundred. No wonder the tribes wanted nothing to do with the white man! Later, when the Balbina hydroelectric dam led to the flooding of the river basin and approximately one-third of the Atroari-Waimiri reserve, FUNAI had relocated about one-third of their total population in 1987 from the Rio Abonari to branch roads off the BR 174 highway north and south of the Alalaú River concrete bridge.

The highway was finally blacktopped in 1997, but by then FUNAI had sent teachers and linguists to teach the Indians their own language and how to write it. They had also provided for the Indians' basic health needs such as vaccinations and dental services. These Indians now have modern facilities and even their own buses with government help, and use video cameras to get a lawyer and sue the government if anything goes wrong. A huge mining operation found minerals on their reserve and the royalties and other aid moved these Indians up to and beyond their counterparts in the white man's world.

In early 2011, Bennie and Theresa drove north on the high-speed asphalted BR 174 to Presidente Figueredo, a huge tourist city on the banks of the rocky rapids of the upper Urubú River. The site was just jungle when Bennie had been asked to fly there in 1972 and 1973; since then, the Balbina dam had formed a vast reservoir, opening a popular vacation spot. The city edges the southernmost boundary of the Atroari-Waimiri Reservation.

As the DeMerchants sped along the highway, they could only marvel that the purpose of their visit was to inaugurate a new church building. The central church the DeMerchants preached in that day had plate glass doors and a steep, sloping auditorium-like floor. Two more UPCB churches in this city help support an ABI.

Bennie was keenly interested when a pastor who came from one of the churches near the Atroari-Waimiri reserve claimed they were reaching some families in these ex-wild tribes. The Indians had seen photos taken in 1974 of their old leaders with him, Theresa, and their two young daughters, Beth and Pam. Those leaders had become a legend to their tribe, but the photo of them with Bennie and his family was evidence enough to their grandchildren that he had been there and had been their friend bringing in government medical folks and medications when the government restricted foreigners in working directly in these areas.

Although the effort by the UPCB to reach these tribes has not waned, neither has the opposition by various groups who have energetically discouraged contact with the UPCB people. Boa Vista, the capital of Roraima, the state directly north of Amazonas, is five hundred miles north of Manaus and provides the headquarters for some of these opposing groups.

In 2014, the DeMerchants flew to Boa Vista to attend the district ABI graduation and convention. Bennie asked a couple in the church there about the work down on the edge of the Atroari-Waimiri reserve. He learned from this excited couple that they had nine students and a couple of new churches right on the edge of the reserve about seven miles south of the Abonari bridge where Indians walked a long way to church. They even had one Indian student at the Bible school. However, Bennie learned that the opposition flew all the leaders from the Mapueira area and brought others by land to Boa Vista to orient them against the UPCB. It worked for a time. One student of the nine quit, and other church members who walked so far to be in the services were pressured to drop off.

Later in the year, some leaders in the church in Manaus drove to Boa Vista for a visit to the Bible school. On the way, they passed directly through a major part of the Indian reserve. They discovered that roads branch off the main asphalt and penetrate the area. One road ninety miles into the jungle east of the main road had twenty-four wooden bridges that crossed the small streams in the area before getting to the tribal people that they had visited in 2013.

Many years ago a simple chorus claimed that "everything that's not of Jesus shall come down." It seems to be quite a paradox: people who spend their lives converting others to Christ, who cast out devils and preach healing in the name of Jesus, refuse to use the name of Jesus in baptism, preaching against it and claiming it is of the Antichrist!

Bennie recently told a worker that the blocking of the Atroaris and Waimiris is only temporary, and suggested a way to beat that: "All we have to do is arrange for twenty kilograms of basic food stuffs free each month for a while for the Indians to come to our place where we have an ABI just a couple hundred feet off the reserve and they will come to pick it up," he explained. "Invite them in for coffee and tapioca cakes. We'll just cast our tapioca cakes on the water. Eventually it will come back."

In 1973, upon seeing the mayhem and murder at the outpost and not knowing the reasons behind the Indians' wary distrust of the white man, Bennie had wondered, *Will we ever be able to reach such treacherous, murderous people with the saving, life-changing gospel of Jesus Christ?*

The most amazing, the most absolute "It has to be God" wonder is slowly happening among the descendants of the Atroari-Waimiri, the tribes that had killed Gilberto. By faith, the haunting question is being answered with a joyful, thankful, resounding "Yes!"

The parking lot at Mapueira, Wai-Wai Indian village.

Look What the Lord Has Done

It's an amazing thing, an astonishing thing, an astounding, staggering, indescribable thing, a wonderful, marvelous, stupendous, and beautiful thing to watch God at work. In the Amazon, He uses two blue-and-white floatplanes, a multitude of aluminum canoes and houseboats with people to fly, paddle, row, and motor them, and He plants them in the nooks and crannies of this vast water- and-jungle tropical basin where they sprout, grow, and produce much fruit. Except for Canutama County, all the other counties in Amazonas State have at least one UPCB. Eight hundred churches line the rivers and river towns in the Basin, while another five hundred churches spread over the rest of the country, thirteen hundred in all.

Major cities such as Boa Vista to the north, Tabatinga to the west, Cruzeiro do Sul and Rio Branco to the southwest, Rio de Janeiro and São Paulo to the south, and Belém to the east radiate out from Manaus like spokes of a wheel. They in turn, however, often serve as hubs for many churches in their respective areas. For example, Tabatinga is the westernmost city in Brazil along the Solimões, the main branch of the Amazon above Manaus. An international border cuts down the street, and one can go back and forth without a passport stamp if not going any farther than Leticia, Colombia. Across the river to the south is the easternmost point of Peru. A large church in Tabatinga serves as a base for works being started behind an island to the south in Benjamin Constante and farther up the Javari River in Atalia do Norte.

Bible Schools: Next to the floatplanes, the Bible schools throughout the country have contributed most to the move of God in Brazil. In 2015, 124 Bible schools all over the country have a combined enrollment of 2,367 students. Understandably, the largest Bible school is in Manaus. In Manaus last November, 141 graduates walked the Jerusalem Convention Center aisle, 99 from the school in Manaus, and 42 from other schools in Iranduba, Novo Airão, Presidente Figuredo, and Rio Preto da Eva, all connected by paved roads. Anticipating an enrollment in 2015 of 400, the Manaus ABI started in early January in air-conditioned classrooms with 50 students in each and still has two classrooms in reserve.

Theresa sends teachers into new areas in the Amazon Basin to start schools where no training exists. After their two-year cycle, some schools in rural areas close down and wait for the next generation to mature. Sometimes within two or three years the school begins again. In larger constituency areas ABIs go constantly. The army of trained young men and women are aggressive and know what we believe and defend it well, creating strong opposition by those churches that do not teach this Jesus Name truth.

The Bible school training has proved so valuable to the work that no one can get a license in the UPC of Brazil now without a graduation certificate from one of the 124 ABIs in the country. This rule was passed by the General Board of the UPC of Brazil in the middle of October 2014. They found that this unifies the work, doctrine, teaching, preaching, and standards, and makes it much easier to work together. Their experience had been that 90 percent of the ministry-related problems they faced had come from the 10 percent untrained workers.

All the students work hard and want to make the grade. Starting in 1972 in Rio with Robert and Jean Norris and including all the other Bible schools in Brazil, nearly ten thousand graduates have swelled the ranks of qualified bearers of the Jesus Name message. As a result, missions are booming. Santa Catarina State had one ABI three years ago: now it has seven. All seven have leadership imported by the missions program from Amazonas State.

Opposition: The whole state of Pará is very strongly Trinitarian Pentecostal. However, Belém in Pará State at the mouth of the Amazon River has a number of churches and preaching points in the suburbs. Now divided into two districts, North, with Belém as its capital, and South, with Maraba as its center, the work there is growing fast.

Bible school teachers were sent to help in Pará in 2011. Some just moved in and stayed there the whole year. The DeMerchants were surprised to find that one teacher who had not communicated with them had eighty-nine students in the Ituperanga area. Even without their training being complete, many of the students already work with groups they preach to. In 2013 the DeMerchants sent a couple to Macapá, capital of Amapá State, to get Bible school training and have heard they are doing well. The leaders realize they are waging a spiritual war and they just go in and work, humbly preaching and teaching the Word to whoever will hear.

One group that has worked for years with the Indians is working hard to stop the UPCB entering into those areas now with Bible-school-trained workers. The linguistics societies translated the Bible into the Indian languages after long decades of living with them in primitive conditions, getting down on paper the vowels, consonants, and other complexities of the language. Along comes the UPCB with their special planes that can easily land in hundreds of places wherever water flows. Well-supplied, trained workers start preaching with an interpreter. Then the airwaves start to crackle!

"These people are of the devil!" messages to the tribal heads declare. "Don't listen to them. They are false prophets. Don't baptize a soul till we get someone there to teach you better the way to be baptized."

However, those well-taught workers have a voice in the jungle! Using the tribe's own Bible, they point out the apostles' way of doing things and a toehold is established.

"Once people believe, we baptize them ASAP," Bennie says. "They connect us with the Word. These people believing in the Word who have their own language in hand can throw a loop to these follow-uppers who want to switch them back."

One of their Wai-Wai leaders asked the translators, "Our own Bible that you translated shows some disciples of John the Baptist being rebaptized in Jesus' name by the apostle Paul and receiving the Holy Ghost speaking in tongues in the nineteenth chapter of Acts. If that is false, how come that is in their Bible and ours that you translated?"

Such questions leave red faces and cause great frustration and fear that they might lose the whole tribe and decades of work to the Oneness, nontraditional, evangelical Pentecostals moving into the area. The Trinitarian Bible translators do not believe what they translate in regard to the message of salvation so clearly shown in Acts chapter two.

Jerusalem Conference Centers or Centro de Convenção Jerusalem: The Jerusalem Conference Center, built in 2005 to accommodate 5,000, has been expanded by two wings, Judea and Samaria, and now provides a place for 10,000 worshipers. With two hundred churches in the Manaus area using it for a variety of meetings, it is already too small.

Churches in other cities, seeing the advantage of having their own center for worship, prayer, Bible school graduations, and conferences have built their own "Jerusalems":

2. Manacapuru—built; capacity 3,000.
3. Itacoatiara—built; capacity 4,000.
4. Eirunepé—under construction, ready for roof; capacity 5,000.
5. Boa Vista, Roraima—lot bought.
6. São Paulo—has a lot at the orphanage; plans to build.
7. Porto Alegre, Rio Grande do Sul State (extreme south)—has a lot, and is making heavy payments.
8. Mossoro, Rio Grande do Norte—under construction.
9. Fortaleza, Ceará State—is buying a lot.
10. Curitiba, Paraná State—bought a lot and are building.
11. Coari— searching for an appropriate lot.
12. South Pará—getting property to build on.

Jubilee Orphanage: São Paulo is the most populous metropolitan state in Brazil with about forty-five million souls and offers a tremendous challenge to a couple dozen UPCBs. Kenneth and Isabel Cooper (she is Brazilian, married to an American in the USA and has worked several years with Mark Hattabaugh in North Miami) were able to register a non-governmental organization (NGO) for a children's home called Jubilee Orphanage to work with street kids in Marinique, São Paulo State. Northwest of the city about a forty-five-minute drive, this huge rural setting sports a church where they have services and an ABI from which they graduated their first sixteen students in November 2014, with Mark Hattabaugh and ministers of São Paulo District and others present. Brother Hattabaugh's enthusiasm bubbles over in the email he sent Bennie in 2011:

> By now you realize the huge impact of your vision and passion that is so far reaching. For years, you've had this burden to see the southern part of Brazil to catch on with the fire of the Amazonas District. Well, God is answering your prayers.
>
> This week the Coopers have made the offer, are clearing the paperwork, and checking on the title of the property adjacent to the orphanage. This property is to be used as the Jerusalem South of the IPUB. Yes, you will now be able to see in the South what God has been doing in the North. I can't tell you how excited we are along with you and the church in Southern Brazil!
>
> I know you had many concerns about the work the Coopers would be doing, how they would fund, and any impact it may have on the congregations IPUB South. Well, here's another way God has used them as an answer to prayer!
>
> The location seems to fall right (perfectly, as God would have it) in the center of that whole district. Easily accessible to all the churches in the area. We plan to make it as Jerusalem, but eventually a place for youth camps and convention center where we can also house and feed people. At this time the churches in the area are paying US $20,000 per three days of meetings. We could be saving all this and using these funds for our own place and for construction/upkeep of our own facility.

Well, seems God has big plans too—not just His kids! Please let me know any suggestions you have for our team to proceed there. I can't wait until you and Brother Crossley and others get to come see this whole area. The location is gorgeous rolling hills and lovely trees. The fact that it is right next to our orphanage makes it easy for us to keep eyes on the property and not need a person to live there, since we already have custodians on location.

When we went down there in March, we were so impressed by the spirit and attitude of the church there. The leaders are sooooo excited! I can tell you this "orphanage" was a much bigger picture in the plan of God than serving children. It has been a huge positive impact on the churches and pastors. We are not asking them for any funds—God has wonderfully provided us with funds from many sources to accomplish this—but what we are seeing is how this is unifying the whole region. I was so amazed and continue to be with emails and reports from these pastors and leaders. All I can say is wow! And thank you, Jesus!

So Pai, get your boots on. Let's go down together and see this lovely place. When you and Brother Crossley go down, you will find the lodging there superb. Wonderful beds, clean house, and great shower. The peaceful atmosphere will surround you. Well, let's just say you have to be there to see it all!

Sister Isabel loves kids—especially street kids—and wants to build up this impressive site encompassing two small ponds between the hills with three main foci: a

Jerusalem Campground, an ABI with dorms, including a large area for parking, and the orphanage compound with a fine expanse for kids to run and play. They have built two residential buildings for teachers and the Coopers. This great vision will take years, step by step, to finish with larger buildings as they grow and bring on more helpers. A good flow of AIMers comes to Brazil and stays at the orphanage outside of São Paulo, one hour northwest driving from the city.

Compassion Services: A few days before Christmas 2014, Bennie had their ABI secretary buy big fiber bags of clean, used bulk clothing. They repacked these into about twenty-six smaller jute bags and he flew eight of them to the Wai-Wai Indian village way back on the rocky Mapueira River. The load included a supply of dried foodstuffs he bought from a huge wholesale warehouse. Including pilot and fuel, the cargo on the 206 went well over seven hundred kilograms, and the plane roared a long time before lifting off into the air. The plane cut northeast for two hours and twenty minutes over the jungle. Bennie could hardly wait to see the Indian people line up for the things he had brought that they needed. The word goes around to other tribes of what was brought, so their mouths also water for Bennie to go to them. Bennie strongly favors first serving those of the household of the faith once delivered to the saints; to do otherwise would make him an infidel. Bennie wonders if they are buying people off to be baptized in Jesus' name into the church. He doesn't know, but he is commanded to cast his bread upon the waters—hopefully in their case, the rivers of the Amazon—and it will return after many days.

The Challenge: The UPC of Brazil today is the work of fifty missionaries, including wives, since 1957. The national church constituency now numbers nearly 140,000 in all Brazil. The DeMerchants remember arriving in Manaus at night on an old four-engine VARIG airlines propeller plane from Belém on October 29, 1965. Not knowing anyone or even where they would sleep that night—and worst of all, not knowing Portuguese—was like flying in the dark with the fuel tanks hovering near empty. In those early days, Bennie would rub shoulders in this city of then 180,000 to 200,000 and pray that they would be saved. Today Bennie can't go downtown in Manaus, a city of 2.5 million, to buy anything without running into some church members in and out of stores or on the street. But the DeMerchants really believed God had a people to be saved here and that He would help them, so step by step they just plugged away. Victory came and people believed as His Word was preached. Now they are requested to be in more church dedications all over, including Manaus, than they can honor. God multiplied trained workers to them, and a great church has begun.

Notice the word *begun*.

In 2013, Brazil crossed the two hundred million population mark. Three hundred cities in Brazil have a population over 100,000, and about 900 cities with over 50,000. The church rejoices over the 100 cities of 100,000 souls where one or more churches carry the banner "Igreja Pentecostal Unida do Brazil." Hundreds of churches in smaller towns and in rural, jungle, river backwaters, lakes, and creeks bear witness to Jesus' name. Oodles of churches are starting up, and many opportunities are sprouting among new Indian tribes. However, two hundred cities in Brazil that have a population of over 100,000 souls still have no messenger. The UPC of Brazil is into less than 20 percent of these places. The challenge remains and is as strong as ever: reach into the other 80 percent for Jesus' name.

At the DeMerchants' debriefings at Global Missions, the officials keep talking about retirement for them even though the DeMerchants never mention the subject. Bennie and Theresa feel that if health-wise they were broken and unable, or if Bennie were talking to his umbrella instead of spitting out fourteen items of data for a flight plan on VHF radio to an air traffic controller after liftoff till acquiring five hundred feet altitude so he can see the plane well on radar, they would readily and gladly quit.

"In the dust of someone else we would say we gave the wagon our push so now it is up to them, and let them do it," Bennie declares. "But to the present, the call of God has not left us and with reasonably good health, we'll plug on.

After all, Moses was eighty years old before he really got started."

ABI graduates and teachers in 2014

"Jerusalem" Convention Center, Manaus

Daniel McKillop, of Plaster Rock, NB;
Global Missions Director
Bruce Howell and his wife, Diane; and author
Dolly McElhaney in Manaus,
July 2015

Theresa and Bennie DeMerchant
Fiftieth Anniversary Celebration, July 2015

About the Author

Delores (Dolly) McElhaney, a graduate of Apostolic Bible Institute, Macalester College, and Tennessee State University, began writing when Jesse Norris recommended her to Edna Nation, a children's editor for Word Aflame Press Sunday school literature. Subsequently, over four hundred of her stories were published. She has penned four other books: *Born with a Mission*, in conjunction with Carl Adams; *Angel at My Shoulder: The Agnes Rich Story*; *Faith Brings an Empty Basket*, coauthored with Jack Leaman; and *Full Throttle*. She has also worked as a freelance copy editor for Thomas Nelson Publishers. For eight years she wrote articles for The Print Out, a bimonthly magazine produced by the Public Relations Department of the then Nashville State Technical Institute, and edited and proofread most of the material published by that school during her employment there. She lives with her very understanding and supportive husband, Bill, in Cookeville, Tennessee.